Debashish Dey

ADVANCE PRAISE FOR
MANAGING AT THE SPEED OF CHANGE

"*Managing at the Speed of Change* will take some of the uncertainty and mystery out of what you have to do."

—JAMES K. BILL
President, CEO
Travelers Express Company
Inc.

"*Managing at the Speed of Change* provides meaningful insights into change dynamics and useful guidelines on change implementation. It may well become the management textbook of choice for coping with future shock."

—ROBERT A. LUTZ
President
Chrysler Corporation

"This book is must reading for anyone involved in managing change. Daryl Conner's *Managing at the Speed of Change* gives organizations the ingredients for becoming winners versus losers through seasoned insights into human behavior and a carefully designed architecture of change management."

—RICHARD W. ZBOROWSKI
Vice President, Human
Resources
R. G. Barry Corporation

"If organizational change is to be anything more than an interesting topic of conversation, the connection between the human being, the change itself, and the organization must be understood. Many write about change, but few have addressed this connection with more clarity than Mr. Conner in *Managing at the Speed of Change*. This is where the rubber meets the road."

—FRANK MELLON
Team Leader
Dow Corning Corporation

"Daryl Conner's explanation of change in today's corporate environment and the role leaders play in the implementation of major change is enlightening, insightful, and encouraging. Highly recommended reading."

—DR. SUSAN SIEGEL
Vice President, Management
Development
Marine Midland Bank

"Change is a major obstacle for some to get over in order to make progress. This insightful book should help."

—DREW LEWIS
Chairman, President, and
CEO
Union Pacific Corporation

"A book of necessity for those who embrace the need for change."

—CHARLES A. SMITH
Executive Vice President
Chase Manhattan Bank, N.A.

"If you only want to talk about change, find a politician. If you want to make change a reality, get a copy of *Managing at the Speed of Change*. And keep it close at hand, for it will guide you through both the rough and good times."

—ROGER KAUFMAN, PH.D.
Professor and Director
Florida State University

"*Managing at the Speed of Change* is the tip of an iceberg that we ignore at our peril. This book and the associated MOC methodology represents the only practical solution we have encountered to equip every line manager with the skills to understand the prevailing, but often unseen, patterns in the flow of change and to succeed in an environment where change is constant and accelerating."

—WOLFGANG E. GRULKE
CEO
Business Futures Group
South Africa

"If you're initiating major change, prepare yourself by taking two aspirin, reading Daryl's book, and getting plenty of rest. Our change effort was (and is) painful, but Daryl's principles have helped us deal proactively with the stress."

—CRAIG E. WEATHERUP
President and CEO
Pepsi-Cola North America

"Daryl Conner is today's authority on major organizational change. His models are understandable, applicable, and elegant. This book captures and effectively communicates both his ideas, and the range and depth of his worldwide experiences with change. Every manager and consultant will find it extremely helpful."

—DR. SANDRA F. JEWELL
President
Jewell Consulting Network,
Inc.

"Anyone who reads *Managing at the Speed of Change* will be compelled to make these principles a permanent part of their professional work and even their personal lives. Daryl Conner's principles and strategies for managing change have been vital to our success in obtaining and maintaining sponsorship for a large-scale change effort in education."

—DAVID F. SALISBURY
Associate Professor
Florida State University
Center for Educational
Technology

"Daryl Conner brings a true blend of wisdom, compassion, and practical experience to the understanding of change and how to manage it. He presents real tools used by the real winners in real organizations to successfully accomplish major change. I'm delighted to have had the opportunity to use his tools—they do indeed work."

—JACK W. STEELE
Information Systems Security
Policy and Resources
National Security Agency

"What makes this book so fascinating is that it not only gives professionals a structured and, above all, very practical approach to change, but it also deals with human behaviors, feelings, and emotions. Daryl R. Conner demonstrates that people can go beyond the boundaries of their abilities if they accept and learn about their resilience."

—WESSEL GANZEVOORT
Deputy Chairman
KPMG Management
Consultants Europe

"Daryl Conner demystifies change management with clear processes and vivid concepts that have stood the rigor of the marketplace."

"A very insightful book into change that is at the top of our reading list for organizational leaders. We are integrating this 'intellectual capital' into our approach of assisting clients to effectively implement major change."

"I am confident that the most effective way of 'managing at the speed of change' is actively preparing oneself, both intellectually and emotionally. Read this book and you will accomplish both."

"The key executive skill of the 90s will be managing change, and Daryl is, in my judgment, the undisputed guru of the change management movement. Every executive who is attempting to manage change can significantly benefit from this offering."

"Daryl Conner has captured in one book the hard and soft issues of successfully managing change. *Managing at the Speed of Change* contains the keys to cope with the rapid changes we are all facing in today's world."

—HYLER BRACEY, PH.D.
President and CEO
The Atlanta Consulting Group
Co-author of *Managing from
the Heart*

"An insightful book for those leaders who wish to maintain a competitive advantage in the 90s and beyond. Daryl Conner provides a wealth of insight into the study of change management that can equip those experiencing major change within their organization with the tools to steer them through turbulent waters. A must for those who wish to capitalize on the advantages inherent in every change opportunity."

—H. TED BALLARD, PH.D.
Consulting Psychologist
North Atlanta Psychological
Associates

"This spirited and original study should cement Daryl Conner's reputation as an anthropologist of transition. With revealing anecdotes, consistently shrewd analysis, and a wealth of practical advice, Conner shows managers how to surf the wave of revolutionary change that is transforming business and government."

—JAMES P. PINKERTON
Counselor, Bush-Quayle '92
Washington, D.C.

"There are many of us today in the field confronting the 'beast' of large-scale organizational change. Our success to date, whether the beast manifests itself in acquisitions, mergers, or business reengineering, has been spotty. Conner has opened a significant door to our future success by defining the construct of organizational resilience. It is now up to us to apply it."

—DAVID SUTHERLAND
Principal
CSC Index

"Daryl Conner's *Managing at the Speed of Change* gives great insight into potential solutions for the new leadership challenges, especially those impacting my most valued asset—the people."

—ROBERT D. CLARK
Vice President
AT&T

"Daryl Conner offers invaluable insights and guiding principles for managing change in a world where increasingly complex problems emerge faster than ever."

—WILLIAM E. MILLIKEN
President
Cities In Schools, Inc.

"The challenges that businesses face today are dramatic, complex, sweeping—and to a large extent familiar. Daryl Conner explains how to successfully deal with change and all its far-flung implications."

—CHARLES GARFIELD,
author of *Second to None: How Our Smartest Companies Put People First*

"Daryl Conner undoubtedly knows more about a systematic approach to organizational change than anyone else in America today. In this book, he shares insights gained from his wealth of experience in working in change situations throughout the world. His identification of organizational resilience as a key capacity for organizations to absorb change in today's world is a major contribution to our understanding of how to work with the future. *Managing at the Speed of Change* is a must for any manager concerned with responding to the changing world environment."

—STEPHEN A. RHINESMITH
President
Rhinesmith and Associates,
Inc.

"Mr. Conner has condensed a wealth of experience in the art of managing change into a book which examines the crux of the issue. With the concept of 'resilience,' Mr. Conner explores the human response to change and offers a number of conceptual models and principles which improves our capacity to understand the change process and to reduce dysfunctional behavior relative to change."

—HOWARD BOWENS, PH.D.
Asst. Professor of
Management
Department of Management
and Organization Science
Wayne State University
Detroit, Michigan

"Daryl Conner has created a virtual handbook for those of us managing change. His insight is compelling. Ignore this book at your peril!"

—LAWRENCE FOX
Deputy Commissioner
Connecticut Department of
Labor

"*Managing at the Speed of Change* is required reading in the decade of downsizing in American industry. Daryl Conner explains how to combine the intuitive skills of a master entrepreneur and the experience of a highly successful CEO in an extremely interesting work!"

—KEN HILL
President
PDX, Inc.

"*Managing at the Speed of Change* offers profound insights into the nature of resilience, and the patterns and principles that underlie change. Whether you are leading change, implementing it, or are simply its victim, Daryl Conner's powerful models and techniques will help you build resilience and navigate the treacherous territory of organizational change management."

—VAUGHN MERLYN
Partner
Center for Information
Technology and Strategy
Ernst & Young

"*Managing at the Speed of Change* concentrates on how to develop resilience in both people and organizations through the use of synergy, culture, commitment, and process at both the micro and macro levels. It is a useful tool in assisting people to identify the various change options and mechanisms that influence their lives."

—ALAN O. TONKIN
Group Human Resources
Executive
Barlow Rand Limited
Sandton, South Africa

"*Managing at the Speed of Change* is a very timely book, and an essential resource for leaders and facilitators of organizational change. It provides a practical, insightful road map for developing a vital competency—organizational and personal resiliency."

—RONALD M. COWIN
President
Cowin Associates, Inc.

"*Managing at the Speed of Change* is fascinating reading. What a tremendous force for good. This book will have a definite positive impact on people's lives both by defining issues and by making those issues manageable. *Managing at the Speed of Change* is like the pebble dropped into the pond. The ripples will touch many lives."

—NANCY HIGHTSHOE
President
Nancy Hightshoe Seminars,
Inc.

"Slowing down the rate of change in our fast-moving world is simply not an option. Increasing our ability as individuals and as organizations to assimilate more and more change faster *and* stay effective is the answer. In this book, Daryl Conner offers valuable insights and practical constructs on how to do this—in his terms, how to increase resilience to organizational change. His prescriptions will be extremely valuable to anyone who finds they are managing 'in permanent white water.'"

—DONALD M. ARNOUDSE
Vice President
CSC Index, Inc.

"Wonderfully vivid in its verbal imagery. Intensely practical for use in every phase of our business. The concepts presented in this book have become our rallying point for enlightened change management. I consider it an indispensable guide to change within any organization."

—MARK G. BARMANN
Executive Vice President &
Chief Information Officer
Charles Schwab

"Having a good idea is only half the story—the more important half is getting the idea implemented and reinforcing its use throughout an organization. That's where this book excels."

—WILLIAM C. BYHAM, Ph.D.
President and CEO
Development Dimensions
International
author of *Zapp! The Lightning of Empowerment*

"Learning to manage change proactively is probably one of the most fundamental skills a manager must have to position himself and his organization on the scale that goes from survival to market leadership. *Managing at the Speed of Change* is an outstanding set of practical principles to help managers at all levels effectively cope with the increasingly changing environment."

—MAURICE CAZES
Executive Development
Consultant
IBM Brazil

"Daryl Conner's methodology around change management empowered me with a framework, language, processes, and tools that apply in virtually every personal and professional situation. The systematic application of this point of view and process increases personal and organizational effectiveness by orders of magnitude."

—Gloria J. Gery
President
Gery & Associates

"By providing the reader with insight as to why and how individuals respond to changes on a personal level, Mr. Conner also helps us anticipate and manage the common responses people have during organizational change. *Managing at the Speed of Change* provides an excellent blueprint for success in managing change. This work is destined to become the classic reference for implementing and managing change."

—Beverly Wright Page, RN
Director of Nursing
Emergency Services
Bronx Lebanon Medical
Center

"Success—even survival—today requires ongoing change. The challenge of a leader is to be a positive instrument of change. Many researchers talk in theory about leading change. Daryl R. Conner's book provides insightful observations and action steps to enable a leader to understand and implement the principles of effective organizational change. This provides the foundation for capable leaders to make a difference."

—David A. Cole
Chairman
Kurt Salmon Associates, Inc.

"Daryl Conner understands that the fabric of an organization is woven by its people and their interactions. He provides a framework for reweaving today's organizations to meet tomorrow's challenges."

—Brian Gorman
Deputy Director
AIDS Resource Center

"I have been teaching Daryl Conner's change management methodology for over ten years at the University of Massachusetts. This course has been one of the most highly sought after and valued by master and doctoral candidates of organization development. I have seen students from many backgrounds and walks of life take this methodology and use it in a variety of professional pursuits. This experience has empowered them to put Daryl's principles into practice."

—Norma Jean Anderson, Ph.D.
Professor, Organizational
Development
University of Massachusetts

"I've learned to trust only those revelations about managing people that I can confirm with my experience in the forest. Daryl Conner's research has revealed insights about change that are just as true in the wild as in the corporate setting, i.e., animal life does not alter its patterns of movement unless it is threatened. Then it goes through periods of confusion until new paths through the forest are determined. Mr. Conner's book shows us that this same phenomena carries forward into boardrooms and companies around the world. *Managing at the Speed of Change* is a must on this year's reading list."

—Thorton W. Morris
Attorney
Thorton W. Morris and
Associates

"Rapid Change is the new status quo. *Managing at the Speed of Change* provides leaders with the strategies they need to successfully manage organizational change both now and in the future."

—DANIEL BURRUS
Technology Forecaster, and
President, Burrus Research
Associates, Inc.

"Without energy the university could not exist. Energy is change. Existence is change. If we do not adjust to change we will not exist. How we recognize, prepare, and adjust is what this 'changing' book is about. Read it and leap into your ever-changing future."

—MILO O. FRANK
author of *How to Get Your
Point Across in 30 Seconds*

"Daryl Conner explains the nature of change in a model that we can apply to our personal and organizational lives. His deep personal knowledge of the subject and fluid prose style helped me move easily through a very complex subject."

—JAC FITZ-ENZ
President
The Saratoga Institute

"Conner has expressed some very real and basic issues senior officers must address to prosper in uncertain times. It's stimulating, insightful, and written for today's business leaders."

—STEWART TURLEY
Chairman of the Board and
President
Jack Eckerd Corporation.

MANAGING

··

AT THE SPEED

··

OF CHANGE

··

MANAGING AT THE SPEED OF *CHANGE*

How Resilient Managers Succeed
and Prosper Where Others Fail

DARYL R. CONNER

VILLARD BOOKS   New York   1993

Library of Congress Cataloging-in-Publication Data

Conner, Daryl.
    Managing at the speed of change : how resilient managers succeed and prosper where others fail / by Daryl R. Conner
        p.   cm.
      ISBN 0-679-40684-0
        1. Organizational change—Management.   I. Title.
    HD58.8.C652   1993
      658.4'06—dc20   92-20753

Text design by Levavi & Levavi, Inc.
Manufactured in the United States of America

9   8   7

Some say that we reveal the unanswered questions in our lives by the nature of the things we try to teach others. This is certainly true in my case. For close to twenty years, I have served others as they attempted to accommodate major transitions. This, of course, reveals my ongoing personal pursuit of unresolved issues about change as well.

Change is often perceived as a perplexing jungle that many people, organizations, and even whole societies enter only to become entangled in the undergrowth of confusion and dysfunction. I have guided people seeking a path through this jungle in several different ways: first as a counselor to troubled individuals and families, later as a consultant to organizations in transition, and now as the head of a research firm disseminating findings about the human response to change.

Regardless of the roles I have played, there has always been an implicit contract between myself and those I serve. In exchange for passing on to them whatever knowledge I possess about managing change, I require that their situation be an opportunity for me to explore new territory and to advance my own understanding of change.

In this respect, I consider myself a perpetual student of human transitions. My clients pay for my tuition, and in return what I give them is a summary of what I have learned and guidance about how these findings may be applied to their situation.

Change is filled with mystery and revelation as well as danger and opportunity. I never promise people who seek my direction that I have all the answers. I offer only the experience and insights that I have gained from many years of assisting others as they have searched for their unique path through the dense and convoluted underbrush.

Nor do I promise people that my way is the only way to navigate this jungle. Some assume human transition is a complex phenomenon that can only be comprehended by an intense study of each and every angle. Others believe that if all the numerous paths of change are studied, it is unlikely that there will be time left to take any one of them to its ultimate point of development; specialization is called for by this group.

The serious student of human change must at some point decide which of these two options best suits his or her needs. You can become a generalist who pursues diverse viewpoints in order to gain a more comprehensive picture of change. Or you can become a specialist in a particular view of change in order to follow it as far as possible.

While both options are valuable, many years ago I chose the second one for two reasons that still hold true for me today: First, I believe it requires long-term, concentrated attention through a specific lens to discern the more subtle lessons a particular perspective can provide. Second, I believe this more focused approach results in the building and continuous refinement of more powerful application tools than would otherwise be possible.

The key is to remember that the lens I use and the subsequent findings it has uncovered represent only one of many possible approaches. Human change can be viewed from numerous perspectives. This book should be read within the context of the many other publications on this same subject. Rather than attempting to refute the findings previously reported by others, my desire is to build on the value of their work and add another viewpoint on the management of change. True understanding of how and why people successfully change is possible only by integrating all the various approaches. I offer this view as my contribution to such an integration.

In this book I share what I believe to be true about people changing. I am aware, however, that everything I have written here cannot be empirically verified. Our investigation is far from complete and much remains to be learned about how to measure some of the factors described. What I can offer is an honest and accurate portrayal of my experiences with change and the successes I have witnessed through my work.

ACKNOWLEDGMENTS

Since this book is about the lessons I have learned as a result of my years of guiding people through the jungle of change, I would like to thank all the clients and professional associates who made those journeys possible. Some of these relationships lasted only the length of a specific project but nonetheless generated important findings for me; others have become long-standing sources of inspiration and encouragement.

I want to also express my appreciation to the wonderful group of people who make up the staff at ODR. This book would not have been possible without their logistic and emotional support, intellectual insight, and willingness to share the lessons they have learned from serving our clients during change. Special mention is due to the ODR Product Development and Research Team. Ernest Clements, Stacie Hagan, Linda Hoopes, Jim Hunt, Mitch Kotula, and Charlie Palmgren provided an important intellectual backboard off which I could bounce my ideas. They are my harshest critics and most challenging audience, which makes them extremely valuable to our joint pursuit of excellence.

Heartfelt gratitude goes to my agent Margret McBride for her belief in this book when it was no more than a leap of faith. And to Emily Bestler of Villard Books, acknowledgment for contributing her editorial talent to the manuscript and her guidance to me during my first journey into the book publishing jungle. Many thanks also to Jeff Davidson for his considerable assistance in the early formulation of the book's conceptual framework, and to Brad Bambarger's phenomenal editorial skill in translating my rather awkward way of stating things into a flow that most people can hopefully understand.

A most sincere appreciation is due Deborah Jolly for accomplishing what must have appeared to her to be an unending task—inputting the many drafts and edits this manuscript has endured. Her skill, patience, and devotion to this effort is unparalleled in my experience.

Finally, it is to my family that I owe my greatest debt. I thank my parents for their most precious gift—life—and all the wonderful experiences it has provided me. To my sons Bryan and Chase, I am grateful for the opportunity to fulfill a longstanding dream that I thought I had lost—the privilege of being a dad. To Michaelene, who has multiple assignments of best friend, love of my life, coparent, and business partner (all cleverly compacted into the role of wife) goes my deepest admiration and appreciation. Everyone who thinks they work hard needs a reward—thank you, Michaelene, for being mine.

CONTENTS

....

PART IV ONE PLUS ONE IS GREATER THAN
TWO   181

How do resilient people gain energy during change rather than feel depleted by it, and why are synergistic relationships the soul of a successful change effort?

PART V   THE NATURE OF RESILIENCE   217

What are the characteristics that separate resilient people from those who suffer from future shock, and how can resilience be fostered in people and organizations?

PART VI OPPORTUNITIES AND
RESPONSIBILITIES   263

What are the responsibilities that come along with learning how to increase human resilience to organizational change?

EPILOGUE   279

INTRODUCTION

I believe this book will fundamentally shift the way you view change in your organization and dramatically increase your capacity to manage projects involving transitions of any type. That's easy for me to say—I know what's coming. You are, however, the one who must decide whether reading this book will be worth your time. To speed your deliberation, allow me to anticipate and answer three basic questions: Why did I write this book? What are my credentials? And what will you gain from its contents?

WHY I WROTE THIS BOOK

As I draft this introduction, I am flying from one war zone of change to another. It is Friday, May 1, 1992. The last image I had of the United States was the news coverage of the rioting taking place in Los Angeles. Ostensibly, the mob was responding to the unexpected not guilty verdict of four white policemen accused of brutality in the widely publicized videotaped beating of a black man. My destination tonight is Johannesburg, South Africa, where I will enter another flashpoint. Ostensibly, this pocket of turmoil is the result of a commitment to dismantle generations of minority white rule over a black majority.

Without negating the racial implications of both situations, I suggest there is another way to interpret these events. The world we live in is showing signs of complexity that our traditional response methods cannot adequately deal with. There is more than tension between blacks and whites going on here. These recent events can also be interpreted as the symptoms of people who are no longer capable of adequately coping with the amount of unmet expectations and change they face.

We cannot afford to distance ourselves from the rioters we see on our TV screens. Those individuals captured on film represent only a small portion of a growing constituency much closer to home than most of us are comfortable admitting. They are but the tip of an iceberg of humanity displaying dysfunctional behavior because they are unable to absorb the magnitude of confusion around them. They are the vanguard of a growing population unprepared to meet the unexpected.

Closer to home there are people within our organizations who are daily falling further behind in their capacity to adjust to change. Just as the fear and irrational behavior caused by rioting immobilized an entire city, our organizations are faltering because of mergers, reorganization plans, new technology, downsizing, or shifting corporate cultures. The challenge for a growing number of organizations today is not that any one of these changes needs to be adjusted to but that several such transitions—sometimes all of them—are occurring at once. Although the dysfunction we see in our organizations may be less dramatic than TV images of rioting and looting, ultimately it is every bit as costly.

There are no safe havens. Yesterday I was in Atlanta delivering a speech to several hundred AT&T executives about how to manage their workforce when an avalanche of organizational change is compounded by social upheaval of violent proportions. Tomorrow in Johannesburg, I am consulting to the senior management team of one of the largest financial institutions in the country, Standard Bank, as they struggle to build the human infrastructure to support the business and social changes unfolding in their part of the world.

I wrote this book because I spend most of my days with executives and managers who are grasping for a way to provide leadership in work environments that are growing ever more turbulent. What you read here will provide needed guidance if you are trying to manage some aspect of an organization caught in the grip of a chaotic world.

MY CREDENTIALS

I'm one of those people who figured out early in life what I wanted to excel at doing. As a result, I have had the time to become exceptionally skilled at doing it. Although my education and early work experience have been assets, the expertise I have developed is due primarily to the long-term focus I've placed on this effort. Whether it is playing the piano, tennis, or the stock market, dedicating one's energies to a single reference point for time periods measured in decades allows mastery at a level not otherwise attainable. This explanation is the most eloquent rationale I have for spending nearly half my life studying when, how, and why people change within organizations.

For the past two decades, I have been immersed in the study of a single phenomenon—the human response to major organizational change. During this period, I have not been merely interested in organizational change, occasionally becoming involved in a few change projects, or studying change along with many other areas of interest. Since 1974 there has been only one, exclusive channel for my professional energies—learning everything I could about why people accept or resist changes affecting their work. Few people have witnessed more change in more organizations, in more industries, in more countries than I have. I believe what I have learned from all of this and have written about in this book can be of use to you.

What I hope will make reading this book particularly interesting is that in it I will show you how to apply what I have learned to your own organization. I will not be presenting a newly formulated "theory" of organizational change; instead, I will discuss what actually works based on my years of observing people all over the world successfully implementing major transformations.

If you're like most managers, you have grown tired of watching a good performance by some self-appointed guru. With today's demands, you need to learn to replicate what works and incorporate it into your own skill base. I have written this book to help you accomplish just that.

There is something else about me that may help you determine if this book will be worth reading. I'm an entrepreneurial-based researcher, which means I have no benefactors to provide a financial safety net. This has a direct bearing on how I present the information you will read.

The entire time I've been conducting my research, I have supported my efforts solely by teaching people how they can use what I've learned to successfully implement important changes within their organizations. This funding arrangement has forced me to remain close to the pulse of what really matters to people as they try to cope with change.

As a researcher, it is easy to lose sight of the practical value of what is being studied. This loss of focus often leads to findings that are academically sound but not very useful to a manager responsible for actually implementing a re-engineering project or new technology. Worse, sometimes organizational research produces results that are extremely relevant to day-to-day struggles with change, but there is no motivation for the researcher to be concerned about packaging the findings for immediate and widespread use. In these situations, we see new insights about change buried in obscure journals or written in books that only other researchers and change specialists understand.

I believe there is a healthy tension associated with knowing that my mortgage will not be paid unless someone finds immediate, practical value in the observations and lessons I offer. Being an entrepreneurial-based researcher means I must put at least as much effort into making sure that my findings can be widely understood and used as I do into determining the meaning of the data and observations I have collected. This reality-based perspective will prove useful to you as you read this book.

WHAT YOU WILL GAIN

If you are responsible for helping to increase the quality and productivity standards in your organization, but the people you manage seem less able to assimilate change than ever before, this book will help you identify a path to your objective. The problem to be addressed here is that too many transitions are occurring too fast. The solution is to increase *resilience* in yourself and those you manage. Resilience, the ability to demonstrate both strength and flexibility in the face of frightening disorder, is the internal guidance system people use to reorient ourselves when blown off course by the winds of change. I'll be practical as I describe the structure you can use to understand resilience, and I will be specific when discussing the principles to follow in applying what you learn.

Success in today's complex markets and work environments requires that many skills be incorporated into the manager's bank of resources. Managing change is only one of these skills, but it has become among the most crucial. Included in the following chapters is a framework you can use to add this skill to your arsenal.

I now invite you to join me in what I regard as the more important learnings from my experience with change.

Part I

THE
SPEED OF
CHANGE

CHAPTER 1

RESILIENCE AND THE SPEED OF CHANGE

*T*he mathematician and philosopher Alfred North Whitehead once observed that "the major advances in civilization are processes which all but wreck the society in which they occur." We live in times that reflect such turmoil. Never before has so much changed so fast and with such dramatic implications for the entire world. From the nuclear family to nuclear-arms treaties, our way of life is transforming as we live it.

At a personal level, change is intensifying dramatically for us all. We face an unsettling amount of individual change as evidenced by the alarming frequency of marriages, pregnancies, divorces, promotions, job changes, relocations, health problems, drug abuse, retirements, and family strife in our society today. Women juggle marriage, children, and careers; men are trying to be sensitive husbands and fathers after skirmishing on the corporate battlefield. In the workplace we are also confronted with massive change—ever-advancing technologies, mergers, acquisitions, rightsizing, new policies and procedures, reorganizations, and constantly shifting duties and reporting responsibilities.

Besides changes at the individual and organizational levels, there are profound national and global transitions that are not only altering our lives but shaping those of our children and grandchildren. For example,

- The primary mode of communication has shifted from typography to electronics, thus changing the way people think, converse, and educate themselves.
- Advanced media technology means that a significant shift in one part of the world is almost instantaneously known on the other side of the globe.
- The growth of information is occurring so fast that the "shelf life" of facts and technology has been reduced to almost nothing.
- The planet's fragile ecosystems will no longer sustain humankind's capacity to reproduce, its increasing demand for natural resources, or its generation of waste.
- Nations bordering the North Atlantic Ocean are no longer the dominant economic and political forces in the international arena.
- Advances in health care and genetic engineering promise new ways of fighting disease, but they also open a Pandora's box of ethical issues.
- Faster modes of transportation are becoming available, creating greater economic opportunities, but with potentially severe psychological and environmental costs.
- The redefinition of traditional male and female, ethnic and racial roles is reshaping the structure of our society.

PURSUING CHANGE

The magnitude of change today can prompt a doom-and-gloom vision, or it can be seen as an opportunity for a fundamental shift in how we humans define ourselves, where we are going, and how we will accomplish our goals. I have chosen the latter option. You can, too. You can make a difference in the course of events affecting you and your company today and in the future by learning how to better manage change.

Consulting to large organizations all over the world as they strive to alter key aspects of their operation has been a rich source of information for me. These engagements have afforded me the opportunity to observe, record, and analyze the behavior of thousands of managers as they attempt to implement major changes, including restructuring for competitive advantage, introducing new technology, shifting to a culture focused on quality and customer service, and many more.

When my work in this area first began to take shape in the early 1970s, it looked to me as if there were plenty of theories already available on the topic of organizational change. But I was interested in going beyond theory to find a way to understand what really works. I felt that the best way to approach this task was to actually witness people attempting to change and to record what I saw.

Much of the research I have conducted is similar to that of field anthropologists and primate specialists. For years, the famous naturalist Diane Fossey lived in the jungles of Africa studying the behavior of gorillas. When she first began to present her findings, she didn't claim to have discovered a new theory of how gorillas behave; she simply offered the results of her observations regarding how they lived.

Instead of going into the jungles to study apes, I have spent much of my life in corporate hallways observing and recording how humans respond to change. What I have acquired from nearly twenty years of consulting, training, and research is a way of understanding what people are actually *doing* when they successfully implement organizational change as well as a way to pass this information on to others.

When I first began to study the behavior of people in transition, my work was limited to the United States, and I assumed that my findings reflected only the American approach to change. As I began to assist companies in Canada and Mexico, then throughout Asia, Australia, Western Europe, South America, and more recently Hungary, Russia, and South Africa, I noticed some striking similarities in how people across the globe address transitions. Wherever I went, I recognized the same phenomenon— *executives who successfully implement change, regardless of their location, display many of the same basic emotions, behaviors, and approaches.* Those who succeed in New York or Moscow operate the same way as winners in Paris or São Paulo. And executives who fail to implement their change initiatives fall into similar traps whether they are in Hong Kong or Sydney.

People within each country demonstrate certain cultural idiosyncrasies in the way they respond to change, of course, but the basic human reactions to change are the same in everyone. By focusing on these similarities, I have found that certain actions fall into patterns, and that these patterns form a structure for understanding and describing the change process. Viewing change as a phenomenon that has a distinct shape and character, and studying individuals and organizations who manage major change well has enabled me to synthesize the key elements of various successful change efforts. In doing so, I have determined that the single most important factor to managing change successfully is the degree to which people demonstrate *resilience*: the capacity to absorb high levels of change while displaying minimal dysfunctional behavior.

After several years of working independently, it became apparent that I had taken my interest in change as far as it was possible for one person to pursue alone. Further investigations of change would demand a formal research vehicle. In 1974, I formed ODR Inc. (Organizational Development Resources), a research-and-development company dedicated to the study of how humans respond to major changes. ODR examines the dynamics of human resilience, advising people who can use our findings to deal with the process of assimilating change in their lives and within their organizations.

Instead of viewing change as a mysterious event, we approach it as an understandable process that can be managed. This perspective allows people to avoid feeling victimized during transition; it promotes confidence that change can be planned and skillfully executed.

The aim of this book is to share what ODR has learned about resilience in the face of change in the hope that this knowledge will help you not only manage your own transitions successfully, but those of others as well.

MYTHS ABOUT CHANGE

From day care through college and the working life beyond, organizations have an immeasurable impact on how we view ourselves in relation to change. From our experiences in school, church, the military, and the many other organizations that touch our lives, most of us have come to accept similar unconscious assumptions about organizational change. Although firmly held, these assumptions are based mostly on fears and prejudice rather than fact. Here are some of the more popular myths:

- It is impossible to understand why people accept or resist change.
- Bureaucracies cannot really be changed.
- What leaders say about change should never be confused with reality.
- Change will always be mismanaged.
- Organizational efficiency and effectiveness inevitably decrease when changes are attempted.
- Those who help you implement the changes in which you believe are heroes, and those who resist are villains.
- Management is inherently insensitive to problems caused during the implementation of change.
- Employees are prone to resist any change that is good for the business.

This kind of unconscious indoctrination is so widespread that most people think it is natural for organizational change to be poorly handled and fail. To the contrary, our research indicates that badly handled organizational change is not the inevitable outcome of flawed human nature. It is merely the result of deeply ingrained habits, and these habits—even when present in one generation after another—can be modified.

People can be redirected to see successful organizational transformation as a distinct possibility. The victimization lessons most people learn from their change experience can be replaced with a real sense of empowerment, which stems from the application of certain guidelines that foster resilience.

The sheer amount of time people spend at work and the impact their jobs have on their lives makes the workplace an ideal location for the development of resilience skills. One of the most effective ways to help people develop the necessary resilience for not only surviving but prospering during major change is to provide implementation guidelines that can be used in the office. In effect, one's place of employment can become a classroom for learning the basics of resilience, which can then be applied not only at work but to other aspects of life as well. For these reasons, this book will present organizational settings as one of the best places to teach and learn resilience skills.

FOCUS ON LEADERSHIP

Because of the seriousness of today's change-related problems and the great potential for opportunities, it is essential that as many people as possible learn how to better assimilate major transitions. This challenge is best approached, however, by focusing on those in leadership positions.

The changes required for the human race to live and work at a continually higher level of productivity and quality demand a critical mass of support from people at all levels of society. Only through the efforts of those who hold positions of formal or informal influence—leaders—can outdated methods of change be cast aside and new behaviors and procedures embraced.

Effective leaders are capable of reframing the thinking of those whom they guide, enabling them to see that significant changes are not only imperative but achievable. Yet the challenges facing these leaders go beyond determining *what* needs to be done differently. They must also address *how* to execute these decisions in a manner that has the greatest possibility for success. Leaders must keep in mind that the accuracy of decisions alone can never compensate for poor implementation.

This book does not focus on what should be changed in the world or which mechanism leaders can use to make the right decisions. Rather, it centers on how managers can fully implement their visions within the time and budget constraints that they face.

If you are someone who influences or hopes to influence organizational change, the mechanisms of resilience addressed in the following chapters will help you be more effective at managing these transitions. But these same mechanisms can be used to foster individual and social change as well. Specifically, this book is for:

- Those who influence personal change: parents for their families, counselors for the troubled, individuals for friends in need.
- Those who influence organizational change: executives, managers, and union leaders for work settings; administrators and teachers for educational systems; clergy for religious institutions; administrators, doctors, and nurses for health-care systems; consultants for their clients.
- Those who influence large-scale social change: politicians for the general public; civil servants for government; political action groups for special interests; researchers for the scientific community; opinion leaders for the media.

PATTERNS AND PRINCIPLES, NOT RULES, ARE THE KEY

This book is based on the lessons learned from observing people exhibiting resilience to major change. These lessons have been fashioned into a set of eight patterns and many principles that can be used by those who have responsibility for influencing and carrying out key decisions involving change in a business environment. Briefly, the eight patterns involve: (1) the nature of change, (2) the process of change, (3) the roles played during change, (4) resistance to it, (5) commitment to it, (6) how change affects culture, (7) synergism, and (8) the nature of resilience. Described in later chapters, these patterns depict how people typically operate during change, and the principles listed at the end of each chapter illustrate how to enhance resilience to change. If you apply these lessons and guidelines, it is possible for you to significantly increase the likelihood of implementing your own organizational change successfully.

Human transformation is too complex to be described by a set of rigid laws. Change is not a discrete event that occurs by linear progression; rather it unfolds on many different levels simultaneously. Instead of relying on hard and fast rules that can get you into trouble, acknowledge the complexity of change by focusing on these patterns and principles for your direction. They provide a much more realistic guidance system because they allow for the subtleties and paradoxes inherent in the way people experience real life.

Understanding how to use these patterns and their principles is essential if you are to successfully manage change. Applying them will help you reduce the problems of resistance in the office and even in your personal life as well as help you dramatically increase support among those involved in major changes. The principles will provide you with a set of powerful guidelines for enhancing the resilience of individuals and organizations. Whether the change you wish to implement is a new approach to marketing your product or a merger with a large company, the principles you will need to apply are the same.

Putting into practice what you learn will not make you immune to the demands of change. Nevertheless, applying this knowledge will enable you to achieve some specific advantages. You will be able to:

- understand that change is not as mysterious as most people think;
- realize that change typically unfolds in a manner that can be recognized and predicted;
- anticipate how you and others will respond during change;
- plan how to implement change;
- recognize the critical symptoms that can help you guide the change process;
- take specific actions to facilitate progress through the change process; and
- help yourself and other people recover more quickly and effectively from the effects of change.

MANAGING AT THE SPEED OF CHANGE

Light travels through space at a constant 186,281 miles per second. The laws of the universe dictate this speed with no deviation. Humans travel through life without the benefit of a fixed velocity. We move at a variable rate that fluctuates according to our capacity for assimilating new information and influences. How well we absorb the implications of change dramatically affects the rate at which we successfully manage the challenges we face, both individually and collectively.

When our perceived abilities and willingness to accomplish a task exceed or fall short of the dangers and opportunities we encounter, a disruption in our expectations results. When this disruption is significant, major change takes place. Just as some people walk faster, think quicker, or show emotion more easily than others, so do people assimilate change at different rates.

Each of us is designed by nature to move through life most effectively and efficiently at a unique pace that will allow us to absorb the major changes we face. This we refer to as our *speed of change*.

When we assimilate less change than our optimum speed would allow, we fail to live up to our potential. When we attempt to assimilate more than our optimum speed permits, we get into trouble. The fastest speed of change is that of an individual progressing through transition. Organizations tend to move more slowly, and the human race as a whole evolves at the slowest rate.

Regardless of age, position, wealth, status, motive, or desire, no individual, organization, or society can adequately absorb life's inevitable transitions any faster than their own speed of change will allow. People can face an unlimited amount of uncertainty and newness, but when they exceed their absorption threshold they begin to display signs of dysfunction: fatigue, emotional burnout, inefficiency, sickness, drug abuse. People whose lives are challenging, but productive and healthy, are typically staying within the bounds of their individual and collective speed of change.

In this book I describe patterns and principles that can be used to accelerate the speed at which you can manage disrupted expectations for yourself and others. There is a basic axiom by which we all operate regardless of whether or not we are conscious of it: **Our lives are the most effective and efficient when we are moving at a speed that allows us to appropriately assimilate the changes we face.** This is not just the velocity at which things around us are changing, but the pace at which we can recover from disrupted expectations. This is not the speed at which we wish to change, or how fast our spouse, boss, or government tells us to change. It is the speed at which we are able to absorb change with a minimum of dysfunctional behavior.

As the world grows more complex, the pressures mount for us to manage more change at increasing speeds. *Managing at the Speed of Change* was written to provide executives, managers, and supervisors with an understanding of the patterns of change and the principles of resilience they need to grasp in order to reach their organizations' optimum speeds of transition. Hopefully, the application of these lessons will help you influence not only your organization's ability to absorb change, but your own assimilation capacity and the capacity of the larger social arenas in which you participate.

INFORMATION FLOW

A brief outline will help you understand the book's flow. The introduction to resilience and the speed of change (Part I) is presented in this and the following chapter. Although the book's focus is on what leaders can do to better manage organizational change, let us not forget that at the heart of the matter are real people with real feelings. The second chapter explores the fear and anxiety that grip us at a personal level when we come face to face with major change.

Chapters 3 and 4 in Part II, The Change Imperative, discuss the increasing impact of change, future shock, and the price to be paid if we don't learn how to absorb change more effectively. In Part III, Lessons Buried in the Mystery, the patterns of change and the principles of resilience start to unfold. Chapters 5 through 10 detail the first six of the eight patterns and their respective principles.

Because of its powerful impact on the other patterns, the seventh pattern dealing with synergistic teamwork is described in detail in Part IV, One Plus One Is Greater Than Two. Chapters 11 and 12 review key lessons drawn from people we observed who form strong, synergistic working relationships to face change.

In Part V, The Nature of Resilience, the eighth and most

important pattern is discussed. Chapters 13 through 15 are devoted to the mechanism of resilience itself—how people can learn to accommodate ever-increasing rates of change without suffering from its debilitating effects.

The book's conclusion, Part VI, Opportunities and Responsibilities, is dedicated to the challenge of going beyond the benefits associated with managing change. People who learn how to become more resilient must also shoulder the obligations that accompany this advantage.

CHAPTER 2

THE BEAST

*I*f our speed of change is the optimum rate at which we can assimilate the transitions in our lives, what happens when we are overwhelmed by more change than we can absorb? Or when our rate of absorbing change is well below that of the people and events around us?

When people can no longer deal successfully with the amount of change in their lives, they begin to display dysfunctional behavior. Later, I will focus more on dysfunctional types of reactions to change and provide examples from real organizational situations. But first, I want to describe what it *feels* like at a personal level to be dysfunctional in the face of change. Possibly you can relate to some of the fears I experienced when I could not adequately assimilate changes in my own life.

EARLY ENCOUNTERS

For many people, having to confront gut-wrenching, whirlwind change is a fairly recent phenomenon. For others like myself, it has been a lifelong struggle. My adult interest in change actually began to form during my childhood.

Throughout my youth, my family moved at least once and often twice a year. These relocations were always emotionally difficult for me, and the fear and distress I experienced were intense. For me, the moves represented more than just leaving one home for another.

It seemed that we were stationary just long enough to adjust to a new routine, surroundings, and friends, and then we were uprooted once again and transplanted to a new location. Some of the treks were down the road to the next town, some to the next state, some across the country.

My father was a success at many things in his life, but business was not one of them. Most of these departures involved a fast exit to stay one step ahead of the creditors. We would leave town abruptly in the middle of the school year, putting everything we owned except for our clothes in storage until we could afford the moving company's expenses. We then set up camp at a motel while my parents looked for a house or apartment. I would register for the new school the following Monday.

Once we settled in our "permanent" quarters, we would join the local church, which—along with the neighbors and the little league team—eventually brought fresh friendships and the illusion of stability until the cycle began again.

My parents were not insensitive to the emotional discomfort these relocations caused me. When they would announce an impending evacuation, their approach was to tell my siblings and me that they understood how upsetting moving was. Then they would remind us that we always ended up liking the new location better than its predecessor and, besides, this would be the final move.

Although the latter statement became a joke after a few "final moves," I did have to admit that each time my current friends always seemed to be the best I'd ever had. Nevertheless, my parents' efforts to remind me that I had successfully adjusted to previous relocations never alleviated my anxiety about each new move. With each departure, I was convinced that it would be impossible to replace my current cast of friends or successfully compete for a good position on the new ball team.

Each exodus was a psychological shock to my system, but my parents simply attributed this to my not liking my new surroundings. "Trouble adjusting" was a euphemism that they used to describe the dysfunctional behavior that I displayed every time we moved.

None of us knew this at the time, but it wasn't the new environments that were wreaking havoc on my emotions; the change event itself wasn't upsetting me, it was the *implications* the event had for my life. I have come to personify these implications as the "Beast."

For years, the Beast won only minor victories, just enough to establish in a young boy's subconscious that *it* was in control, not I. Every time we moved, I would cry for days, lamenting my lost friends and feeling petrified of the new house or apartment. I would have many sleepless nights anxiously awaiting the inevitable bully in each school.

As I grew a little older, I realized that this nomadic existence was a way of life for my parents and not a series of aberrations occurring since my birth. I finally grew to expect no more than a year's residency in any one location and to even anticipate the stages in the move cycle. I never liked the stages, but once I recognized them, I learned that I could prepare myself for them. New moves then became slightly less devastating.

IN THE GRIP OF THE BEAST

The Beast has a way of determining when it is time for each individual to go beyond the preparatory levels of intimidation and be traumatized into total submission. My early signs of security and courage soon gave way to a heightened sense of anxiety. When I was ten years old, the Beast apparently decided that

I was becoming too comfortable with these transitions and the move-cycle discomfort was no longer enough; sheer terror soon awaited me.

At that time, we moved from a pleasant house in a nice neighborhood in Los Angeles to a wretched hotel in downtown Gadsden, Alabama. My life shifted from playing with friendly, familiar kids on well-kept asphalt playgrounds to dealing with hostile unknowns who wore no shoes in the dirt school yard and pointed at me as they huddled among themselves to joke about my funny West Coast accent. I will spare you the gory details of life for an insecure fourth grader in this radically new setting; suffice it to say that all my earlier move-related distress paled in comparison.

After weeks of being sent home from school every day with a new physical ailment, most of which mystified the school nurse, my parents decided that I might adjust better if I were not in such strange surroundings. So they decided that I should stay with my grandparents, who lived even farther in the country, in the small town of Boaz, Alabama.

To help you truly understand the gravity of the situation, let me relate my perspective at the time. For me, Gadsden, Alabama, had the same relationship to Los Angeles as eating brussels sprouts had to kissing my girlfriend. The move from LA to Gadsden was rough, but Boaz made Gadsden seem like a thriving metropolis in comparison.

I didn't like the town, the weather, the school, my teacher, the kids, the lunchroom, the school bus, the food, the corn fields, the cows, the TV shows, the grass, the air, or the water. I was reluctant to meet other children my age, much less establish any friendships; I was alienated from my parents and hostile toward my grandparents; and I avoided school by again complaining of physical pain in various and often creative parts of my body. Despite numerous visits to the doctor, a medical cause for these mysterious ailments could not be found.

The Beast was pleased—it was winning. I was learning one of my first change-related lessons, unconscious though it was:

When life does not match how you anticipate it will be, the Beast takes control.

In time, I accepted Boaz as a tolerable and, eventually, a pleasant place to live. As I now know, this was possible in part because the Beast sometimes loosens its grip after you pay it homage.

DREAMS BECOME NIGHTMARES

The Beast did not limit its intrusions into my life to changes of only a negative nature. I learned that it imposes its will during positive transitions as well.

My dad's business misadventures were the main reasons that we lived such a chaotic life. The turmoil was due not only to the many physical moves but to the radical fluctuations we endured going up and down the economic ladder. The combination of geographic shifts (which I now think of as horizontal movement) occurring at the same time as the economic shifts (vertical movement) caused a peculiar sort of out-of-control, "gyroscope" feeling that permeated our lives. In spite of all this madness, occasionally the wheel of fortune would come up with a horizontal/vertical combination that was wonderful.

By the time I was in sixth grade, our migration brought us to Nashville, Tennessee. But this time, life took an unexpected turn for the better. After an extended stay at the local motel, we moved to a house—a great house. It seemed like a dream home; it was big, I had my own room, and it came with a swimming pool.

When we went to see the house for the first time, I thought my parents were playing a cruel joke on us. I could not remember a move in which we ended up with a house as nice as this. There was plenty of space in which to play, my own private bedroom (that could be locked to keep out unwanted sisters), and not only a pool but the only pool in the neighborhood. It had everything that I had ever wanted.

I have since learned that it is during precisely these circumstances that the Beast takes great pleasure in demonstrating its skill in the art of camouflage. Apparently, torturing people as they confront the obvious traumas of life can become boring. So the Beast waits for situations such as "the perfect house" to display its stealth. The torment the Beast inflicts is painful, but the revelation that getting what we want can also hurt us makes the results all the more devastating.

Within only a few days of moving in, I realized that I had gotten everything I had ever desired in a new house, and it was killing me. Such is the beastly nature of change. Every up side has a down side: Even seemingly positive change has negative implications.

Big house? What appeared to be plenty of room to run and play during the day became a cold, gray, endless hallway between me and my parents in the dead of night, when I was the only one awake to hear strange sounds. My own private room? It was so private that no one could ever hear my screams should a prowler break in. It would be days before they would find my lifeless body in this isolated cul-de-sac. Swimming pool? It may have passed as one by day. But at night, the lights in the pool reflected off the garage and into my window, revealing its true purpose as a swamplike incubator for unspeakable creatures.

The Beast loves to take dreams and turn them into nightmares. I was able to live in the house of my dreams, but it came with implications for which I was unprepared. Here, I learned another important lesson: The Beast was to control not only negative but positive change in my life.

The Beast's efforts to establish superiority over my emotions during periods of change did not go unrewarded. But these lessons of dominance were of a subconscious nature. I have learned subsequently that the Beast prefers not to reveal itself to its victims at all and certainly not before years of covert education have fully secured its ruling position. So until my teenage years, I had no conscious knowledge of the Beast.

I'M NOT THE ONLY VICTIM

By the time I was in high school, we lived in Pensacola, Florida. At that point, the Beast was so much a part of my life that I never recognized its effects on my own behavior. I did begin to notice something odd in others, however. I became vaguely aware that when people I knew encountered significant and unexpected events such as divorce, loss of job, or pregnancy they became distant, irritable, preoccupied, and unproductive. Instead of just accepting these symptoms as normal reactions to emotional trauma, I began to question why they occurred.

I also noticed that these reactions were not limited to individuals. Groups of people displayed dysfunction as well. When a popular basketball star was killed in an automobile accident at my high school, the team and coach went into shock, spending the rest of the season in disarray. When John F. Kennedy was shot, I witnessed the entire school display collective cognitive dissonance for hours after the announcement.

It was far from a fully developed thought, but I remember sensing that some type of relationship must exist between people who face major, unexpected change in their lives and the decline that I could see in their ability to cope with their environment. Although I wasn't conscious of it at the time, the link between my own dysfunction during change and theirs was beginning to surface. The common denominator was that at these points in time, we were all operating at a speed of change well below that which was necessary to effectively absorb the transitions we faced.

My awareness of the Beast grew stronger, but it had not yet evolved into something that I could consciously acknowledge. My first realization that an inability to cope with change could produce irreversible damage was the day I came home from high school to find police cars and an ambulance in front of our neighbor's house across the street. The two young children had found their mother in the utility room hanging from an electrical cord. The suicide note said something like: "I can't juggle it all anymore." I didn't really know her, and so her death was more of a curiosity for me than anything else. I remember asking myself, "What was it in her life that caused so much to happen so fast that she could no longer 'juggle it all'?" The specifics about her story I never knew, but it was apparent to me even then that she had wrestled with the Beast and lost.

WHISTLING IN THE DARK

Despite these early experiences, it wasn't until several years later that I was able to fully recognize the Beast as a personal adversary. In 1969, I received orders to go to Vietnam. It was only then that I became aware of the relationship between significant, unexpected events in my life and my own dysfunctional behavior.

I had been in the army for less than a year when the notice to ship out appeared on my desk. Everyone in my unit knew that we were likely to go sooner or later. But I learned firsthand that intellectual preparation cannot be confused with emotional readiness.

To fully convey the reaction I had when I received these orders, I first need to describe the ingenious manner in which humans protect themselves from the unwanted. We all have an extensive ability to deny negative realities. When people talk themselves into thinking that they are prepared for an impending negative event, it is usually just a façade to bolster their terrified souls. Like whistling in the dark when walking through a cemetery, the greater the fear, the more effort people invest into portraying calm—as if pretending to be unmoved by frightening prospects convinces the menace to keep away.

We humans develop elaborate mechanisms to keep from focusing on dreaded situations. For example, when confronting their own mortality, most people have a special tune to whistle that helps them repress the terror. Those who are religious whistle a tune of joy because they soon will be walking through the

Pearly Gates of Heaven. Others prefer the hard-nosed tune that life is a crap shoot; when your number is up, it's up—so you might as well accept it.

If other people around us are whistling the same tune, all the better. We are unconsciously reassured by the harmonic convergence of it all. This is why humans have such a strong need to surround themselves with like-minded whistlers: Each provides a reinforcing verification for the others. In other words, expand the number of people whistling your tune and you increase the likelihood of being right.

There is nothing wrong with whistling these tunes or even buying into our own con job to relieve some of the burden that comes with facing great anxiety. In fact, these tunes are a wonderful way to compose ourselves when we are terrified. Problems occur, however, when people seduce, coerce, force, and even kill each other because one group doesn't like the other group's tune or when someone suggests that ours is not *the* tune.

I was twenty-one years old, in the army for six months, and Vietnam was staring me in the face. Everywhere I went I was confronted with the same question: "Are you ready?" Only now can I offer testimony to the two responses that occurred within me simultaneously:

Conscious Dialogue: "Me? Am *I* ready? You must be joking. Of course I'm ready! I thought it all out, and I am totally prepared for any eventuality."

Unconscious Dialogue: "I know the odds are against me, but there's no way *I'll* ever really have to go. If I do, the orders won't come until I'm too close to being discharged for me to be sent; and if I am sent, the war will end the day I get in the country; and if it doesn't, they won't send me into the bush—I'll be working in a psychological unit at a hospital in Saigon; and if I do go into the field to see the troops, it won't be during any action; and if an attack did occur, they wouldn't ask me to pick up a weapon; and if they did, no one would shoot at me; and if they did, I wouldn't get hit;

and if I did get wounded, it wouldn't be serious; and if it was, I wouldn't die; and if I did . . . and if I did . . . no way I'll ever get orders to go; and if I do, they won't come until I'm too close to discharge for me to go . . ."

In an effort to prove (mostly to myself) how prepared I was, I puckered like I had bitten into a lemon the size of a grapefruit and was whistling as long and hard as I possibly could. The name of my particular tune was "Of course I'm ready, I'm a psychologist." I can't claim to have written the original score because everyone in the Mental Hygiene Unit to which I was assigned was whistling the same subliminal tune, day and night.

Every so often, periodic episodes of panic ensued when one of the "protected" actually did receive orders to go. But calm was restored soon after when those remaining began to whistle again.

Despite my diligent whistling, I found the envelope on my desk one morning with the dreaded orders inside. The wrenching sound from my gut must have been a wake-up call for the Beast. Nevertheless, my outward appearance was that of any self-respecting psychological professional who understands the dynamics of human behavior—I was unfazed. I was ready!

Regardless of what I thought was a convincing performance that nothing of consequence had happened, I instantly began to feel a sense of isolation from my colleagues. They continued to whistle the sacred tune, but in doing so they huddled a little closer to each other and a little farther from me each day. This meant the collective reinforcement that I had grown to enjoy was gradually losing its power to protect me. When the combined impact of the choir wanes, you are left with only your own frail attempts to pump up the volume—music to the Beast's ear.

Within days, the Beast had penetrated my inadequate defenses and I was immobilized. Over the next few weeks, vomiting, diarrhea, loss of appetite, insomnia, and overall malaise resulted in a twenty-pound weight loss and a general strike by my body.

Yes, I was ready to face Vietnam—intellectually. The problem was that no one had notified my emotions or my body.

HEAD AND HEART

The human mind can process data much faster than the heart can. People often fail to recognize this, acting surprised that they were not as prepared for certain events as they thought they would be.

This is true for everyone, but those of us who become convinced that all life's mysteries can be reduced to theories are especially vulnerable to surprises. Psychologists are at particular risk because their area of expertise tends to breed a false sense of security. Their downfall is thinking that they are able to understand the mother of all complexities: the human psyche. This makes them more vulnerable than the average know-it-all.

Naïve arrogance increases the impact when you get slammed by change. I thought that I had all the answers because I held a degree in psychology. But the Beast rendered me physically incapacitated while I desperately clung to the intellectual illusion of readiness. This duality within me set off a body-versus-mind war for the next several months while a typographical error in my orders was being corrected. I finally received new orders from headquarters rescinding the first set of orders. Much to my relief, this meant that I didn't have to go.

Of course, I was pleased at the outcome, but both my wounded mind and decimated body knew that the Beast of change was the undisputed winner of my internal struggle. The only benefit was that I was now fully aware of its presence, its power, and its ability to control not only me, but anyone who reaches beyond the confines of what they anticipate and feel prepared for.

THE BIGGER THEY COME

Once I knew firsthand what the Beast could do to individuals, I began to recognize its effect on institutions. While stationed at

Fort Benning, Georgia, I was a member of two teams formed to develop the army's first official race-relations program and formal drug-abuse halfway-house program. The behavioral-science aspect of designing these programs was challenging enough. But we also faced a harsh reality—no one would use them. In spite of what we felt were flawless approaches to these problems, massive resistance formed against the programs.

Acknowledging the existence of race or drug problems, let alone enthusiastically supporting formal strategies to deal with them, was simply not part of the army's culture at that time. I learned from this experience that the inability to adjust to change was not just an individual phenomenon. If the Beast takes pleasure in the dysfunctional behavior of a young boy, imagine the rush it gets when it stops whole institutions in their tracks. But even reducing the level of quality and productivity of an entire organization is not enough. The Beast has a feeding frenzy on the power drain that occurs when whole industries or even entire countries are unable to adjust to new and unexpected realities.

Watergate, the *Challenger* space-shuttle disaster, the collapse of the Berlin Wall, the rise in environmental consciousness—all are major changes, bad and good, that result in significantly unexpected implications. The Beast does not cause these events, but it is always there, hiding, waiting to exploit our inability to adapt to them.

STALKING THE BEAST

Humans are control-oriented animals. Our need for control has driven us to dominate all other known life forms. This need is so strong that as individuals, groups, and whole societies, we invest a tremendous amount of energy trying to understand our environments so that we can better influence the events directly affecting us. We study history, attempt to keep pace with current events, and, as much as possible, project the future so that we can maintain a big-picture perspective on our lives.

Without this perspective, we would be unable to make sense of the world. We would be unable to attach meaning to our experiences or anticipate events and their consequences. The resulting ambiguity would be unbearable for our high control needs, so we do everything we can to make our lives orderly and predictable. Some have a higher tolerance for ambiguity than others do, but we all seek our own level of desired predictability.

Major change minimizes our ability to dominate events. For a species whose entire existence is predicated on its ability to control its environment, the ultimate nightmare is an inability to assimilate change in a world transforming itself faster by the minute.

The Beast is the fear and anxiety within us all as we encounter the significant, unanticipated changes that shatter our expectations. It is not a figment of the imagination, and it cannot be explained away as a passing phase that afflicts only a young boy or a frightened soldier. The Beast is a metaphor, but its devastation of individuals, organizations, and society is real.

I was well into my adult years before I made a conscious connection between the Beast's invasion of my life and the key career decisions I had made: first to become a psychologist in order to study personal transitions, later to become a consultant specializing in organizational change, and finally to form ODR as a research platform to investigate human resilience. Once I realized the Beast could be observed, studied, and possibly understood, it became a focal point of my life. The discovery of a mechanism to deal effectively with the Beast of change has become more than a professional interest on my part; it is an obligation that I and now others are committed to pursue.

To force the Beast into the light of day, we must be aware that, as I mentioned earlier, it is not the events of change that so confuse and overwhelm us, but the *unanticipated implications these events bring to our lives.* Just as broken glass and fallen trees are not part of a hurricane but aspects of its aftermath, dysfunctional behaviors are not the Beast. They are the emotional, behavioral, and physiological scars left behind after a major, unexpected change.

THE CRISIS OF CHANGE

Once we at ODR learned that the key to pursuing the Beast was to focus on disrupted expectations, we began to unearth important insights. For example, we found that the Beast could thrive on positive disruptions as well as on frightening changes. Whenever people's expectations dramatically alter circumstances in ways for which they are unprepared, the Beast can flourish.

A crisis is the point at which it becomes apparent that what we had planned is no longer feasible and our expectations are disrupted. The disruption can be good (winning the lottery) or bad (losing one's job). But if it is a significant departure from what we expected, a crisis ensues because ambiguity enters the situation.

Just as a shark is attracted to the smell of blood, the Beast is attracted to the scent of ambiguity. Again, it doesn't matter if the event is interpreted as positive or negative. The important thing is that you are unprepared for the confusion, disconnection, disenchantment, and anger, or even the enthusiasm, joy, and pleasure that is to follow. **It's not the surprises in life that are so debilitating. The truly crushing force is being surprised that you are surprised.**

Ambiguity is everywhere. Turn on the Cable News Network, walk down your organization's hallways, or go into your son's or daughter's room. Or better yet, just sit right where you are and consider your own anxiety about not being able to control your life as you perhaps once did. How many times this year have you faced a major disruption in your expectations (positive or negative) that left you feeling disoriented, unsure, and less able to solve problems or take advantage of opportunities? In one way or another, we have all experienced the Beast.

This book offers specific information about the patterns people tend to follow during change and the principles that you can use to enhance the latent resilience in you and those whom you manage. By applying these guidelines, you can learn to replicate the actions of successful people who achieve their change objectives on time and within budget. Through learning how to enhance your own resilience and foster it in others, you will be better prepared to protect yourself and your organization from a fast-changing world in which the Beast grows stronger every day.

Part II

THE CHANGE IMPERATIVE

*F*rameworks that have held firm for generations, providing the basic structure for the world as we know it, have started to falter. Fundamental notions about business, science, government, philosophy, religion, and human behavior that have remained relatively stable for decades now don't seem to apply. Traditional ground rules no longer guarantee the results they once did; some may now even prove detrimental. The intricate balance that makes up the web of life is in a state of unprecedented "disequilibrium."

As a result of this disequilibrium, many of the things we used to take for granted we no longer do: the bank you have relied on for years, the background of the people who move into your neighborhood, the values of the people who belong to your church or synagogue, the security of knowing your life savings are safe, the faith you used to place in your doctor and minister or rabbi, the security of your job, the competence of those who manage where you work, the integrity of your congressperson.

Learning the patterns and principles that will allow us to

manage change and increase our resilience is not just a luxury but a necessity. This urgency is based not only on the problems we must solve, but also on the positive visions we feel compelled to pursue. In both cases, we must recognize the cost of failing to absorb the magnitude of change coming our way. Regardless of whether it is problems or opportunities that dictate the circumstances of change, the shifting of basic paradigms generates conditions that can improve or reduce the quality of our lives. Therefore, we have the chance to be either architects or victims of our future.

CHAPTER 3

WELCOME TO DAY TWENTY-NINE

*I*n "The Second Coming," a poem that heralded the Russian Revolution of 1917 and the reformation of the modern world, Irish poet William Butler Yeats proclaimed that the "centre cannot hold." Today, more than ever, people feel the loss of that "centre" and the sense of stability it once provided. Many of the frames of reference that once offered some degree of predictability and order are fast disappearing. The world is changing so rapidly that confusion and dysfunction have become more the rule than the exception.

THE LILY-PAD RIDDLE

A powerful illustration of the exponential effect of change comes not from a scientist or a futurist, but from a child's riddle:

On day one, a large lake contains only a single small lily pad. Each day the number of lily pads doubles, until on the thirtieth day the lake is totally choked with vegetation. On what day was the lake half full?

The answer, of course, is the twenty-ninth day. It takes twenty-nine days for the first half of the lake to fill with lily pads, but only twenty-four additional hours for the lake to become overwhelmed.

Welcome to day twenty-nine. Imagine that the proliferating lily pads represent the expanding array of changes that face the world. Suppose that the human resilience required to address these changes is represented by the lake's capacity to accommodate the lily pads. What happens as day twenty-nine approaches?

New changes occur daily, but people cannot absorb the repercussions fast enough to keep pace. The capacity of the human mind for invention far outstrips its ability to assimilate the changes that inventions produce. What can be done? People are not going to stop creating new problems and opportunities, and the lily pads are not going to stop multiplying.

Let's explore what takes place as the lake is consumed by the multiplying lily pads. In one part of the lake appears the lily pad of diminishing resources, in another part the lily pad of a population growing in some sectors and aging in others. In a cove, the lily pad of advancing technology surfaces and next to it appears the lily pad of economic stagnation. Nearby, global cooperation among governments emerges along with expanding competition for the world's markets. In yet another inlet, we see the inability to dispose of nonbiodegradable garbage and toxic waste.

Some of these analogous lily pads represent positive changes in the world and others, negative changes. Regardless, more surface every day, and each requires assimilation: the emergence of the Pacific Rim as a global economic power; a unified European market; the decline of the industrial predominance of the United States. There are also the newest disease for which we have no cure; shifting, potentially catastrophic weather patterns; and the realization that more and more foods are not as safe to eat as we once thought they were.

Faster and faster the changes come: famine, radical shifts in the major economies, increases in productivity, ecological devastation, heightened sensitivity to human rights and ethnic determination, mergers and acquisitions, reorganizations, new products and markets, escalating drug abuse and crime, fallen heroes, alliances with those we formerly feared, distrust for old friends, education systems that can't educate, political leaders who don't lead. The lily pads continue to multiply, and each one brings with it personal, organizational, and social consequences.

"Don't worry," someone from a boat yells as he or she attempts to navigate the lake. "The channels are still open. Half the lake is totally free of lily pads!"

"Half?" you say. It took twenty-nine days for the lake to become half full of lily pads; tomorrow, the lake will be completely consumed.

This analogy sheds light on how people today face a world of escalating change. Even though the foundations that have provided the structure for civilization as we have known it are shifting beneath us, many people continue to operate as if change of this magnitude can be managed in the same manner that change has always been approached. They say: "Don't worry, it always seems to work itself out."

CHANGE HAS CHANGED

Nearly twenty-five hundred years ago, the Greek philosopher Heraclitus wrote that you cannot dip your toes into the same river twice. In other words, the ancients faced the challenge of transition just as we do today. In one form or another, people have always had to confront the repercussions of change.

So what is different? Isn't the way we experience and adjust to dramatic shifts today much the same as it was in past centuries? Is it any more difficult today than it was a thousand years ago or for our parents' generation? They had to face change, didn't they?

But the change encountered in previous eras was different. What has changed about change is its magnitude, the approach it requires, the increasing seriousness of its implications, and the diminishing shelf life of the effectiveness of our responses to it.

THE MAGNITUDE OF CHANGE

Today, there is more change to contend with than ever before. The volume, momentum, and complexity of change is accelerating at an increasing rate.

Volume refers to the number of changes we have to face. It's higher now than at any previous point in human history. To confirm this, compare a current issue of *The Wall Street Journal* with an issue from five, ten, or twenty years ago. You will quickly see that the number of organizational changes reported has risen dramatically.

We measure the *momentum* of change by analyzing how long people have to implement a change and the length of time before another change becomes necessary. Both of these time frames have notably decreased, which means the momentum of change is increasing.

Meanwhile, the *complexity* of the changes people address today is far greater than in years past. Now marriages often involve children from previous families, and mergers are announced in the middle of the execution of major acquisitions already taking place.

There is no information available to suggest that the growth in volume, momentum, and complexity of the "lily pads" in our lives is diminishing. The current combined weight of these three factors has no precedent and is rapidly expanding beyond our capacity to respond effectively. It is even more sobering to consider that all evidence suggests that the changes our children will encounter will make today's instability seem rather tame.

How is it possible that change can continue to intensify? In attempting to understand this myself, I have focused on seven fundamental issues that seem to be contributing to the dramatic increase in the magnitude of the changes we now face:

1. Faster communication and knowledge acquisition;
2. A growing worldwide population;
3. Increasing interdependence and competition;
4. Limited resources;
5. Diversifying political and religious ideologies;
6. Constant transitions of power; and
7. Ecological distress.

The rate of communication and knowledge acquisition has exploded among a growing worldwide population. This has spawned a combination of more interdependence and more competition as people struggle for access to the planet's limited resources. These resources are being controlled by an expanding number of political/religious ideologies whose degree of cooperation and antagonism are in constant flux. And all of this is occurring in a fragile ecological system that is showing signs of stress as it absorbs increasing amounts of waste and pollution.

Each of these seven issues spawns a great deal of change separately. Then, as they interact with each other, they generate even more change. The result is transformation of geometrically escalating proportions. Although the array of transitions we now confront is staggering, these seven fundamental issues represent the primary categories of "lily pads" that continue to proliferate in the world.

Unbridled change presents unprecedented challenges and pressures requiring responses more sophisticated than we have ever faced before. In tumultuous environments, every solution brings more complex problems—not worse problems necessarily, but ones requiring more creative approaches. For example, the world is not worse off because of the invention of the computer. But even with all the good that these machines have provided, information systems have complicated our lives in unforeseen ways.

Fueled by the interaction of the seven factors, the increases in volume, momentum, and complexity of change have combined to render the environment in which people live and work chaotic. To handle the demands of this massive change, people must radically shift what they think, how they feel, what they believe, and how they behave.

Within organizational settings, these revolutionary changes are reflected in the challenges executives face. For instance, most organizations today are dealing with external pressures from domestic and global competition, unstable economies, government regulation, unions, and consumer groups. They are coping simultaneously with internal pressure for increased organizational effectiveness, productivity, and quality. Such external and internal pressures push management to develop new technology, systems, and human-relations skills.

The changing profile of the work force presents another set of new circumstances for executives. In some industries and regions, today's average worker is younger, better educated, more interested in the quality of life, more likely to be a woman, and less responsive to traditional management tactics than ever before. In other areas, the average worker is older, less educated, from a social minority, and also unresponsive to conventional management tactics. Changing values in the work force, especially regarding compensation, advancement, participation, company loyalty, willingness to relocate, and treatment of minorities and the handicapped require creative management strategies that are both accommodating to individuals and beneficial to the business.

The increasing complexity in delivering goods and services sets up yet another challenge for management. As our world becomes more sophisticated and complicated, the need for innovations in the use of advanced information systems, organizational structures, and improved production methods and machinery becomes evident.

In light of the challenges above, for years ODR has been conducting an annual survey among organizational leaders regarding the changes they consider most crucial to success in business and society. The results from the current survey suggest that most organizations are facing several, if not all, of the tasks listed below:

- Initiating major reorganization plans
- Improving competitiveness through the implementation of total quality-management processes
- Incorporating information systems as an integral part of business and production strategies
- Integrating customer-service mentality and behaviors throughout the organization
- Responding to new or increased global competition
- Accommodating the turmoil associated with mergers, acquisitions, and leveraged buyouts
- Redefining the organizational culture to be more supportive of corporate business objectives
- Initiating cost-containment mechanisms
- Rightsizing the work force
- Establishing employee-involvement programs to generate a sense of empowerment and commitment
- Establishing new products and markets
- Incorporating new production/manufacturing procedures and machinery
- Adjusting to the changing profile and needs of today's employees
- Complying with new government regulations

Trying to implement these myriad changes has brought on mass confusion. Organizations, like individuals, can only absorb so many changes at one time. They then need a chance to recover before they can effectively take on the next change.

CHANGING HOW WE MANAGE CHANGE

Just as star high school athletes often find themselves humbled when faced with college tryouts, humankind now finds itself confronting change of a higher order than ever before. The methods that we used in the 1960s, 1970s, or even 1980s to approach transitions in technology, medicine, or human relations are not enough to manage these changes successfully today. Because the scale of change has advanced, we must alter the way we attempt to manage it.

Suppose you are an executive driving down the road with the corporate gas pedal floored, yet competitors are still passing you by. You are pushing your company toward change as hard as you can, but the car will not go more than 35 miles per hour. You bemoan the fact that your competitors are advancing with ease while you're running your vehicle into the ground just to keep up. Desperately, you look for answers. At the next gas station, you receive some good advice: "At twenty-five miles per hour, shift into second gear. You've done all you can in first gear."

So it is with managing change. First gear has served us well, but it now inhibits our performance. The way we used to approach change is no longer viable. As long as we maintain a first-gear mentality regarding change management, limited results are all we can expect.

The secret to mastering greater levels of change is not to press harder on a pedal already floored. Traditional methods for managing change will not get us very far in today's world. The answer lies in shifting our perceptions toward change and how it is managed.

Organizations, like individuals, have a speed of change at which they operate best. This speed reflects the degree to which the organization can absorb major change while minimizing dysfunctional behavior. Also, an organization's speed of change is a variable that can fluctuate dramatically based on specific circumstances (to be discussed in subsequent chapters). But at any point in time an organization's capacity to efficiently and effectively assimilate the transitions it encounters is limited by its level of resilience, or speed of change. To increase your organization's speed of change you have to look at change differently.

Learning how to view and manage change in a new way is possibly the most important change that you will ever make. The framework for doing this is outlined in the patterns and principles of change that appear in later chapters.

THE INTENSIFYING IMPACT OF CHANGE

In general, we are much more aware of the impact of change today than ever before. For example, there has been a major increase over the last several years in the level of future change that organizations anticipate they will have to confront. We have found that managers' predictions of change fall into three categories:

1. *No change.* There are organizations that believe they face a future of relative equilibrium: Their industries are not in a state of flux, their direct and indirect markets remain stable, and they face little chance of encountering any new meaningful competition. These managers also believe that customers will not increase their expectations and demands, the quality of their products and services is adequate, and there is a low probability that new or upgraded technology will be required. They anticipate no new governmental regulations or policies that will affect business, feel that it is unlikely a merger or acquisition will take place, and are satisfied with the efficiency and reliability of internal business operations.

2. *Sporadic, incremental change.* Because of the problems or opportunities generated by one or more of the above issues, some managers believe that they face a significant, but confined, period of change. During this period, they anticipate that many changes will affect their organizations but that these changes will influence only certain groups at specific times, or they will affect everyone in the organization, but only for a limited time. They predict that once the changes are in place, relative calm will prevail, and people will once again devote most of their energy

to maintaining the new status quo or simply making routine adjustments.

The issues mentioned in this scenario will fluctuate period-ically, so periods of moderate or even dramatic change are an-ticipated. Nevertheless, they expect that periods of relative stability will follow these spikes of change activity.

3. *Continuous, overlapping change.* There are other organiza-tions that are facing many, if not all, of the previously mentioned issues. To them, there appears to be no end in sight to these transitions, and they anticipate having to make substantial ad-justments. They expect the future to bring overlapping transi-tions that form a continuous stream of landmark modifications. These organizations foresee that more time will be spent assim-ilating major change than in taking advantage of periods of equi-librium.

Such organizations believe that many of these changes will not only be disruptive to existing expectations but also extremely challenging to absorb. The transitions that they expect to con-front will require sophisticated planning and sustained effort. They do not view these change demands as short term. Instead, they see the turmoil as representing an era of unending transition.

Over the years, there has been a dramatic shift in how or-ganizations view their future. In the early 1970s, corporate Amer-ica on average was split as follows:

No change: 60 percent
Sporadic, incremental change: 35 percent
Continuous, overlapping change: 5 percent

In the intervening years, there has been a significant reversal of these figures. Today, as I listen to managers all over the world, they report a vastly different outlook:

No change: 1 percent
Sporadic, incremental change: 24 percent
Continuous, overlapping change: 75 percent

People tell us that because of all this turmoil, they are juggling more tasks, more personal problems, and even more opportunities than ever before. We also hear that due to the interrelated nature of these issues, trouble in one area inevitably causes problems in another. As events unfold, there is less time to react, leaving only short-term, tactical maneuvers as options. Often, these knee-jerk reactions cannot adequately deal with the issues; control declines and anxiety increases.

Ever-increasing change is inevitable and will be the hallmark of our lives. The ability to successfully manage change has become one of the most important skills needed for personal happiness, the prosperity of organizations, and the health of the planet. Fortunately, more and more people share this viewpoint. Managing change is now a vital topic of interest for people seeking to enhance their personal or corporate efficiency and effectiveness.

THE SHELF LIFE PROBLEM

Not only are changes multiplying exponentially like lily pads in a pond, but solutions to them have a shorter shelf life than ever before. The programs, procedures, and strategies that we develop to take advantage of new opportunities or solve new problems are becoming obsolete faster than ever.

A story helps illustrate my point: Some coal miners desperately needed to relight a lantern to illuminate their escape during an emergency. One miner was known for always carrying a spare match, carefully guarded in a sealed container. The other miners called to him in the darkness to use his match. They saw no light, but heard him scratching furiously to strike the match. When one finally asked what was wrong, he replied, "I don't know. It should work. I tested it before I put it in the case."

In today's environment, even if you figure out how to absorb the changes you encounter, the effective life span of your change decisions will be shorter than you anticipate. The solutions to your emergencies may seem to have no more duration than the spark of a match; one use and you need a new one. For example, John Sculley, the innovative chairman of Apple Computer, Inc., says that more than half of Apple's revenues comes from products that were not even invented three years ago.

All available data suggest that we are not in the middle of an era of dramatic transformation—we are on the initial edge. Remember when "American-made" meant quality and "Made in Japan" meant cheap? Remember when banks were secure and risk averse, hospitals were safe and affordable, sexually transmitted diseases were cured with a shot of penicillin, marijuana was our primary drug of concern, and computers were big and expensive? It wasn't that long ago.

Mark down the date that you read this book. I can say with great confidence that in three years you will look back on this period as "the good old days" when life was relatively calm.

When I mention at seminars that today represents the good old days, the audience usually lets out a collective gasp, followed by a bit of nervous laughter. They hope I'm kidding, and I wish I were.

Our world as it is now will look slow and uncomplicated compared to what it is sure to become within the next few years: You have more control and less ambiguity today than you are likely to have for the rest of your life.

WHAT TO DO

Given our present capacity to absorb transition, many individuals, families, groups, organizations, industries, and even countries are at the equivalent of day twenty-nine. Soon, we will no longer be able to navigate the surrounding turbulence caused by unresolved problems and missed opportunities.

What is the answer? If we can't stop the lily pads from

multiplying, we must learn to expand the lake's capacity to absorb them. The lake represents human resilience and the ability
to assimilate change. We must broaden our capabilities and dramatically increase our facility for not only accepting but flourishing in constant transition. We must change how we manage
change.

CHAPTER 4
· ·

FUTURE SHOCK IS HERE

*O*ne of the most fascinating consulting assignments I've ever undertaken was a joint effort between ODR and the international consulting practice of KPMG Peat Marwick to train Soviet managers of the Muscovite construction ministry Mosinzhstroi. Now dismantled, Mosinzhstroi was the agency responsible for the building, upkeep, and improvement of Moscow's physical infrastructure. At its peak, it employed more than thirty-five thousand people in the service of the city's construction needs and was part of Gostroi, the former state ministry of construction of the U.S.S.R., which employed 11 million people. In 1990, seventy Mosinzhstroi executives came to the United States for training. They were all bright, well-educated senior managers who were trained engineers and about fifty-eight years old on the average.

Much of our training took place in Moscow, but we provided some of it in the United States not only to expose the managers to modern, high-tech factories and innovative construction techniques but also to immerse them in America's free-market economy. Because this project was part of the former Soviet Union's efforts to move from a centrally controlled economy to one driven by a free market, it was vital to their training that they experience firsthand what it felt like to live and work in an open, capitalist society.

As you might expect, these men experienced intense shock when they encountered daily life in the United States. They had read and discussed the concepts of profit, competition, and multiple options for consumers, but their understanding was purely academic and did not prepare them for a real-life free-market economy.

After they had been here a few days, several of the men remarked that they missed their home cooking. In particular, they longed for some authentic Russian sausage. Rather than purchasing some sausage for them, we took several of the men on their first trip to an American supermarket.

At that time grocery stores in Russia were beyond comprehension—unless you have lived through a hurricane or an earthquake. Store shelves were barren most of the time, but even so, there were long lines for the meager selection of goods. What few items did remain were exactly what you would expect to be left behind: Things you wouldn't want unless you were nearly starving.

For the Russian people, food shortage was a fact of life and has been for generations, with no relief in sight. So we were excited about introducing these men to the bounty of the average American supermarket. We expected them to be like kids in the candy store of their dreams.

They were.

Their eyes lit up at the vast array of food and other products on the shelves. They had money in their pockets, and they knew what they wanted. We had fun watching them find the sausage at the meat counter and become even more excited as they saw how many brands there were from which to choose.

But their excitement soon turned to confusion. In their homeland, there were only two options when buying sausage—

the official state brand or none at all. Making a selection in their stores was simple: You waited in long lines and put up with sometimes unruly crowds to finally get to a counter where you were to tell the clerk what you want. Typically, the request for the desired item was not by brand name because in most cases there was only one provider of each item. Successful grocery shopping was dependent primarily on getting in line early and relying on physical strength and stamina when struggling for position in the often aggressive crowds.

In that suburban Atlanta supermarket, the Soviets were so overwhelmed by the array of brand names, sizes, colors, and flavors that after half an hour they left without buying anything. Even though they were hungry and had the money to buy whatever they wanted, the ambiguity of the situation rendered them unable to make a decision. They left empty-handed.

These executives were in the United States to learn how to make the dreams of perestroika a reality. Yet they were stopped dead in their tracks by a task most Americans consider routine. Their ability to make a decision and take action was overwhelmed by a sausage display in a grocery store; the monumental freedom of choice immobilized them.

Does this mean these executives should return to the dark days of Communist inefficiency to reduce the stress of simple buying decisions? No, they know too much now to go back. Yet they will not be able to take advantage of the dramatic opportunities before them unless they learn how to absorb the impact of change options and decisions with minimal dysfunctional behavior.

TOO MUCH, TOO FAST

Social observer and author Alvin Toffler was the first to popularize a term that described the potentially debilitating effects of major change. In a summer 1965 article in *Horizon* magazine, Toffler first coined the term *future shock*, and in 1970 I was profoundly influenced by his book of the same title. Although he did not directly mention the concepts of resilience and the speed of change as defined here, he accurately predicted the devastation that would result if we were unable to assimilate the changes he foresaw. "Future shock is the shattering stress and disorientation that we induce in individuals by subjecting them to too much change in too short a time," he wrote.

Toffler warned that widespread reductions in effectiveness were coming if we did not learn how to prevent and/or manage future shock. Future shock relates to the overlapping impact of too much change that is too complex to deal with and occurs at too rapid a pace. The results are high levels of stress (manifested by such things as relationship conflicts, ulcers, and even suicide) and the inability to adapt quickly enough (as evidenced by symptoms such as lagging productivity and quality).

Essentially, future shock occurs when people are asked to absorb more disruption than they have the capacity to take in. One outcome is that dangers with catastrophic implications go unsolved. Evidence of today's future shock can be seen in such things as overflowing landfills, inadequate public schools, drug- and crime-infested neighborhoods, a ballooning federal budget deficit, and acid rain devastating our woodlands. Signs of future shock confront the business community as well, with things like the full value of new technology seldom being realized and the desired increase in commitment to quality often being unattainable.

Future shock can result not only from dangers but also from missed opportunities. Once, after conducting a briefing of our research findings for the White House staff, I was approached by a Pentagon official who told me that one of the ways that they were seeing future shock was in the open revolt of fighter pilots against more new technology. The pilots were saying: "Don't put any more technology in my cockpit. I can't keep up with everything, and you're going to kill me."

The pilots were not complaining about bad or unwanted technology. Often, it was technology that they had asked for and even helped design. They were simply saying, "My plate is too full now. Don't bring me any more opportunities. I can't digest

what I have." Still, the Pentagon has vendors constantly solicit-
ing innovations to aid the pilot. Most of this technology is indeed
worthwhile; the issue is simply absorption capacity.

People of all races and nationalities throughout the world are
beginning to realize that the ground rules of the past will not
produce the results they once did. For example, many executives
we have interviewed report that they have no real hope that some
of the promises to shareholders of enhanced customer service or
increased profits can be achieved within the planned time and
budget constraints. Likewise, politicians routinely run on cam-
paign pledges of no new taxes or improved education that they
know they have little chance of fulfilling.

THE HOUSEBOAT FALLACY

Because of the number of positive and negative changes we need
to assimilate, people today are living with more stress, uncertainty, disruption, and insecurity than at any time in history.
Many people have learned to accommodate the stress of increased
change by reducing their expectations for success.

Have you ever been sunburned on a cloudy day? When the
sun is tucked safely behind the clouds, it seems impossible that its
rays are still beating down on your skin. We continue to play
volleyball, swim, or just lie about, thinking we can stay out as
long as we like. Because we can't see the sun, we assume it won't
hurt us. But like the sun, change can burn you even when you
can't see it. Organizations are in danger when they accommodate
gradually heightening dysfunction. Eventually, the heat of
change will grow great enough to burn them.

Meanwhile, the consequences of an inadequate response to
change are more costly than ever. Vince Lombardi, the famous
football coach, once said, "I never lost a game. I just ran out of
time on a few occasions." Given today's challenges, the result of
running out of time is far more significant. For many people,
organizations, nations, and maybe even our entire planet some-
day, there may not be a next season.

The quality of life for not only the next twenty years but for future generations depends on what we accomplish today. How do we explain to our grandchildren that we meant well, but we ran out of time before we established priorities to protect our air, water, and other natural resources, to cure AIDS, to develop an alternative to armed conflict as a means of resolving global differences, to learn how to protect the ozone layer, to reclaim our urban areas from drug barons, or to establish an educational system that adequately prepares them for the future?

The human race is ill-equipped to deal with the burden of major changes already occurring, let alone those to come. Most people today have learned to handle change the way someone would pilot a houseboat on a lake. The houseboat captain does well when there is plenty of room on the lake to maneuver, and there are many protective coves should an occasional storm develop. But today, managers familiar with houseboat-style challenges find themselves in the middle of white-water rapids. Because their only experience has been with navigating calm waters, they tell themselves and their crew that these problems are only a passing squall. "Hang on, things will smooth out soon," they say as dramatic change continues to toss everyone about.

When these managers realize that conditions will never again be "smooth sailing," they issue new orders: "We must become more efficient at what we have always done. Everyone on the houseboat work ten percent faster than you did last year!"

The reality is that an entirely different craft and a new set of skills are required to maneuver safely through rapids. Houseboat captains need to shift their frames of reference about boating if they are even to survive, much less prosper, in constantly churning waters.

SIGNS OF DISTRESS

The working definition ODR uses for future shock is "that point when humans can no longer assimilate change without displaying dysfunctional behavior." Let's focus on the last part of this definition—"without displaying dysfunctional behavior." People don't stop changing when they have entered future shock; they just become less and less effective both on the job and in their personal lives.

After years of observing such situations, we've come to regard dysfunctional behavior in the workplace as any behavior or feeling that diverts resources away from meeting productivity and quality standards. Although this definition is primarily designed for use in organizational settings, it applies to individuals as well. A person's individual productivity or quality of life and that of his or her family are reduced when dysfunctional behavior is present. It is equally true that productivity and quality standards are diminished within a large constituency or even an entire country if change is not absorbed effectively.

Today, we are seeing more signs of future shock and the attendant dysfunctional behavior than ever before. This is a clear indication that people are confronted with more change than they can realistically absorb. There are many symptoms that reflect the varying degrees of dysfunctional behavior, ranging from the inconsequential to the extreme. The onset of future shock, and the accompanying low levels of dysfunction, may be signified by:

- Brief irritation, which may divert attention from work
- Poor communication and reduced trust
- Decreased honesty and directness
- Defensive and blameful behavior
- Reduced propensity for risk-taking
- Poor decision making
- Increased conflict with fellow workers
- Decreased team effectiveness
- Inappropriate outbursts at the office
- Venting job frustration at home

As the seriousness of the dysfunctional behavior progresses, additional psychological and physical symptoms may manifest themselves within the individual, including:

- Feelings of victimization and unempowerment
- Lower morale
- Headaches
- Stomach pains
- Chronic absenteeism
- Apathy or compliance behavior
- Feelings of resignation

An extremely high degree of future shock may result in severe dysfunctional reactions, such as:

- Malicious compliance
- Overt blocking of company tasks or procedures
- Covert undermining of organizational leadership
- Actively promoting a negative attitude in others
- Strike
- Sabotage
- Chronic depression
- Substance abuse or other addictive behaviors
- Physical or psychological breakdowns
- Family abuse
- Suicide

This is not intended as a complete list of all the dysfunctional behaviors caused by change. It merely indicates some of the symptoms seen today in families, businesses, and societies.

SATURATED SPONGES

Individuals experiencing future shock are like saturated sponges. Although already soaked, someone walks in with another two-gallon pitcher of major change and pours it on them. In organizations around the world, change is typically poured onto the physically and emotionally saturated sponges of the work force while management watches helplessly as their intended objectives run down the drain.

Senior executives spend their careers struggling to reach positions of power only to be disillusioned. "I've worked my way to the top; I am making the right decisions and pushing the right strategic buttons. But the lights are not coming on throughout my company. There seems to be a short in the circuitry somewhere. Either the lights don't come on at all when I push the buttons, or they blink off and on, or they light up only while I'm watching."

When you make the right decisions but the lights don't come on, you may be dealing with people who are overwhelmed on a personal, organizational, and/or social level.

A saturated sponge can no more absorb spring water than it can sewage; hence, the *correctness* of ideas or change objectives do not ensure effective response. Across every industry we have studied, senior executives and managers are frustrated because they cannot successfully implement their decisions on time and within budget.

Managers can no longer flip a switch and pour on the changes. The "spray-and-pray" approach (i.e., announcing a major change and hoping that it will take hold) is out of date and insufficient. Instead, managers must carefully orchestrate the flow of change, guiding their actions by asking such questions as: "Where will this change have its greatest impact and at what speed?" "Should we proceed?" "Who is going to absorb it first?" "How do I prepare that part of the organization for what will happen?"

NO TIME FOR DOOM AND GLOOM

In unstable times, attempting to manage the transition process has all the complications and risks of conducting open-heart surgery while the patient is carrying a trunk up several flights of stairs. Many people look at this level of challenge and conclude that the best for which they can hope is a compromised future. Rather than yield to doom-and-gloom forecasts, we should regard magnitudinous change as an opportunity.

The renowned architect Frank Lloyd Wright said, "Man built most nobly when limitations were at their greatest." Meeting the challenges of major change today and in the future requires a fundamental shift in how we view ourselves, what we want to achieve, and how we are going to accomplish our goals.

To prosper, remain competitive, or simply survive, leaders need to respond to a growing number of profound changes in how they govern countries, structure companies, conduct business, use technology, treat employees, and deal with customers. Poor execution of changes at any of these levels will yield costly implications for all of us.

By studying individuals and organizations who manage major change well, we have been able to identify the key elements that allow the change process to succeed. **The main ingredient of success is the ability resilient people have to understand and use to their advantage the principles underlying basic human patterns that operate during change.**

Part III

LESSONS BURIED IN THE MYSTERY

*I*n his book *Fifth Discipline,* Peter Senge asserts that the "structures of which we are unaware hold us prisoner." It is an illuminating statement, one that points to a key theme of this book. Only by understanding how certain variables in our lives relate to each other and how they influence our behavior during transition will we ever reach our optimum speed of change.

People who see change as a mysterious event that lacks structure and a predictable sequence needlessly waste time and energy being confused by reactions that are really quite common during transitions. For example, struggling to suppress the fears generated by ambiguity runs counter to this natural part of the change process; fighting against these fears consumes resources that could otherwise be used to assimilate the change. You will be much more effective if you approach change as a manageable process with definite structures and outcomes that can be reliably anticipated. Behind the apparent mystery of human transition resides a framework composed of both patterns and principles— *the structure of change.*

Life is filled with hidden patterns that operate as riverbeds for the flow of our experience. There are all kinds of concealed patterns to the way people function: A marriage has its ebb and flow of intimacy; a corporation's culture has a rhythm at which it moves through its work; the stock market fluctuates according to cyclical economic forces.

These patterns of operation are invisible to the untrained eye and typically go unnoticed by most people. Yet their influence is powerful and ignorance of their presence is an inadequate defense. Not understanding that a truck is bearing down on you from behind offers no protection from the consequences.

When you demystify an influential pattern in your life, orchestrating your future suddenly becomes possible. Instead of being victimized by these patterns, you can work with or around them, and they can become your allies.

The knowledge that certain events will, in all likelihood, occur at predictable points in the change process allows you to influence what will happen. For example, if you can predict certain emotional reactions to change, you can take specific actions to either encourage or inhibit these responses. If you anticipate why and how strongly a particular group will resist a change in your office before it is announced, you may be able to modify your announcement in some way to avoid or minimize their concerns. For those concerns that you cannot mitigate, you can at least anticipate the reactions people will have and prepare a response.

This way, you reduce the mystery of change for yourself and increase the likelihood that the group being affected will successfully implement the project.

The structure of change consists of the key patterns that reflect how people tend to react during transitions. Most people are unaware of these patterns, and yet they represent the typical knowledge, behaviors, feelings, and attitudes we all demonstrate during major changes. I have identified eight patterns that I believe are the most critical to successfully managing major organizational change. These I'll refer to formally as the *eight patterns in the organizational change process.* Understanding how people have responded, are responding, or will respond to organizational change is possible by accurately interpreting how these patterns unfold within individuals and among groups.

In Parts III and IV of the book, I will discuss seven of these configurations in detail and will describe the mechanisms of human change as patterns that address the following issues: the nature and process of major organizational change, the roles that are central to change, how resistance and commitment are formed, the importance of organizational culture, and why synergistic relationships are so critical to successful change. I will describe the eighth pattern dealing with resilience itself in Part V.

DETECTIVES FOR HIRE

ODR's goal has always been to demystify the hidden dynamics that govern the human transition process in order to foster an architectural approach to managing change. We rely on the information we've gained from many different fields of study, including psychology, organizational behavior, anthropology, world history, physics, and statistical analysis. To pursue our goal, we have also found it necessary to blend the skills normally used in several diverse occupations, including those of researcher, consultant, psychologist, coach, executive, and detective.

The detective skills required in our work serve as a focal point for this section. A detective works with what appear to be unrelated facts, perceptions, observations, inferences, and intuitions to find an explanation for events. A detective looks for order beneath confusion, a flow embedded in frenzy.

Detectives often solve mysteries with nothing more than persistence, attention to detail, and a great deal of luck. They rely on these assets to turn information over and over again, looking for the right combination of factors that will lead to the one pivotal clue that serves as the linchpin for the entire investigation.

We have learned that some of the same skills needed for

basic detective work are also required to reveal the structure buried in the mystery of change. To uncover the pivotal clues in this investigation, we have spent years asking the same question in many different settings and in many different countries: "Why do some people seem to fare better than others in a particular situation when theoretically they all face the same level of crisis?"

When two people live across the street from each other and both lose their homes to a tornado, why does one bounce back from the initial shock stronger than ever while the other's life goes into a tailspin, never to recover? When two organizations seem to confront the same amount of ambiguity and confusion following a sudden downturn in their traditionally strong markets, how does one break from its old paradigm to create a successful new line of products and distribution channels, while the other founders as it attempts to explain its mounting losses and fights to protect its operation's status quo?

There is a category of people who demonstrate a set of characteristics that seem to greatly enhance their ability to absorb major change. Through close observation and interviews, we have determined that some of their actions fall into a distinctly different configuration from the other seven patterns. We call this configuration the resilience pattern.

THE PIVOTAL CLUE

Resilience is the pivotal clue that allows the mystery of change to be reframed into an understandable and manageable process. With resilience serving as a reference point, you can influence the circumstances that surround you, prepare yourself and others to better absorb disruption, and skillfully plan and implement your desired future.

The pliability that resilient people demonstrate and their capacity to rebound after the initial trauma of change allows them to sidestep the dysfunctions of future shock. Rather than becoming victims of change, people who demonstrate resilient characteristics most often prosper during disruption and disorder.

Resilient people face no less of a challenge than others when confronting a crisis, but they typically regain their equilibrium faster, maintain a higher level of quality and productivity in their work, preserve their physical and emotional health, and achieve more of their objectives than people who experience future shock.

Resilient people and organizations are no less susceptible than others to the stresses of change. It's not that they can prevent the disruptive effects of change, but that the effects are ultimately more fruitful and less damaging. They have a much greater capacity for bouncing back quickly after the initial shock.

Inventor, architect, and philosopher R. Buckminster Fuller coined a phrase that Harold Willens expanded upon in his 1984 book on nuclear disarmament, *The Trimtab Factor*. According to Willens, the trimtab theory holds that the "application of even a small amount of leverage can have a powerful effect." In other words, life is filled with innocent-looking minor issues or actions that actually play major roles in the outcome of events.

What if your organization were about to introduce a new technology that would dramatically change the nature of your daily work? During this period, a promotion opportunity could open for which you are perfectly suited except that management sees you as often unable to accommodate deviations from the standard operating procedure. It is unlikely that you would secure the promotion.

On the other hand, what if you lacked some of the intellect and talent of several of your contemporaries, but your ability to perform your job was more than adequate and your capacity to assimilate more change than they with a minimum of dysfunction was a well-known fact. You would probably get the job.

In a fast-paced, continually shifting environment, resilience to change is often the single most important factor that distinguishes those who succeed from those who fail.

THE STRUCTURE OF CHANGE

Although all the basic patterns are important, the resilience pattern is the most critical to successful change. It alone is central to increasing our tolerance to future shock; nevertheless, its effect is strongest when it is fortified with principles drawn from the other patterns.

Of the eight patterns in the organizational change process, the one with resilience as its focus is the *primary pattern*. The remaining seven are *support patterns* because they add strength and resilience to the primary pattern. The primary pattern consists of the key characteristics that form the basis for resilience in an individual or group. In Part V, I will describe this resilience pattern in detail and position it as the cornerstone of the human capacity to absorb change. The support patterns represent seven additional clusters of knowledge, behaviors, feelings, and attitudes that are crucial to the outcomes of organizational change. Related to each support pattern are principles that, when applied, tend to bolster an individual's resilience during change.

The dynamics of human change have a definite structure. This structure is pictured with the primary resilience pattern at the center, surrounded by the seven support patterns (see Figure 1). These support patterns address the nature of change, the process of change, roles of change, resisting change, committing to change, how culture influences change, and the importance of synergistic teamwork. Each support pattern can serve as a source for strengthening the primary pattern by the application of its respective resilience principles. When these linking principles are understood and used in conjunction with the elements from the resilience pattern itself, it is possible to greatly increase your capacity to assimilate change with minimal dysfunctional behavior.

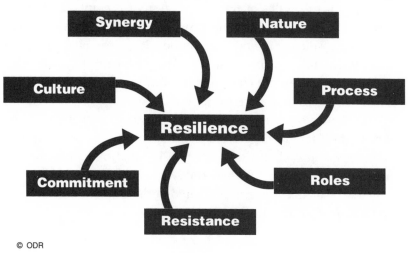

Figure 1

WE'RE ALL IN THIS TOGETHER

The consequences of mismanaged change in one part of the world can directly affect many others around the globe. The success or failure of such efforts as the emerging "new South Africa," the democratization of the former Eastern bloc countries, the structuring of a single European market, and the improvement of public education in the United States will have a profound impact on all people, regardless of how remote or isolated their location. We are, most assuredly, all in this together.

Bruce Laingen, one of the American hostages held in Iran for 444 days, commented on how some people endure such ordeals better than others: "Human beings are like tea bags. You don't know your own strength until you get into hot water." If significantly increasing the resilience of individuals, families, organizations, and entire societies sounds like a formidable task, that's because it is. Without the "hot water" of a prospective future filled with even more change and greater future shock, we may not find the strength and commitment for the challenges ahead.

The future will generate even more ambiguity and chaos than we face today. Learning how to raise our individual and collective resilience is not just a good idea—it is *imperative*. To accomplish this, we *must* uncover the key patterns embedded within the dynamics of change; it is within these patterns that the principles of resilience are to be found.

To help you resolve your own mystery of change, in the next six chapters I will present the first six of the seven support patterns. From each of these patterns, I will also identify the key linking principles that, when followed, will help fortify your primary resilience pattern or that of others and minimize the likelihood of future shock.

CHAPTER 5

THE NATURE OF CHANGE

*T*he *nature of change* is the first of the support patterns. We spend a great deal of our lives matching the capabilities with which we are blessed against the challenges we face. *Capability* here refers to our abilities and our willingness to apply them. An individual is only as strong as the weaker of these two factors. The *challenges* we confront in life consist of the dangers we see and the opportunities we acknowledge.

When the challenges we encounter are matched equally with our capabilities, we are usually able to predict what the outcome of a situation will be. When challenges are greater than our capabilities, this balance is upset and we are usually not able to accurately anticipate what will happen. When our equilibrium disintegrates, our expectations are disrupted and change is at hand.

Perhaps the most interesting thing about observing people's reactions to change is that the same event can be perceived as a negative change by one person and a positive change by another. After nearly two decades of observing this phenomenon, I have often found that whether people perceive a change as positive or negative depends not only on the actual outcomes of the change, but also on the degree of influence they believe they exert in the situation.

We seem to be more comfortable with change when our ability and willingness to change can help determine the outcome of events. The feeling of well-being that comes from perceiving that a change is positive is the result of much more than simply getting what we want. Fundamental to these feelings of comfort is the satisfaction that stems from meeting our need for control.

Change is not perceived as negative because of its unwanted effects as much as because of our inability to predict and control it. Bad events in our lives would not be so unpleasant if we could stop them as they occur or at least anticipate them and then prepare for the consequences. We view change as negative when we are unable to foresee it, when we dislike its implications and feel unprepared for its effects. Thus a critical factor affecting our perception of change as positive or negative is the degree of control we exercise over our environment.

SEEKING CONTROL

Accurately predicting the future helps greatly to reduce the discomfort of uncertainty. It follows then that disrupting someone's expectations about important issues or events elicits a strong reaction.

There are many misconceptions about what constitutes a major change. For example, some people think a change is major if it involves a great deal of money. But we have learned that this is actually a poor indicator of how people perceive change. I have watched an organization spend millions of dollars upgrading their technology, and yet the new system was so consistent with what workers were expecting and prepared for that the change caused only slight alterations in how they anticipated operating, making it a minor change. On the other hand, I have seen the movement of paper clips from one side of the office to the other produce a cultural explosion: "That's not the way we do things around here."

Another misconception is that people only resist change if it involves an event that they dislike. If that were true, then those fortunate, desired events in our lives, like earning a college degree, getting married, or being promoted, would require only minor adjustments. Such is not the case for most people. The degree, the marriage, and the promotion are powerful motivators as we strive toward them and joyful events when they take place, but we soon find that these auspicious occasions create hidden problems of their own.

These kinds of misconceptions make change more of a mystery than it is. It doesn't matter if the change costs a great deal of money or very little. Nor does it matter if it is initially seen as positive or negative. What matters is how disruptive it is to those who are affected. Remember, we feel the most vulnerable to change when we are surprised that we are surprised.

Change is minor when it does not significantly disrupt what you anticipated would happen. In these circumstances, you simply fine-tune your expectations and adapt to the change. Such adjustments are so common and subtle that they typically go unnoticed, leaving the impression that no change has occurred. For example, say that you knew upon accepting a job that you would have to occasionally work late going over reports. You find out that your work load requires you to pull an all-nighter once a month. Working through the night is tough and stressful, but it doesn't disrupt your expectations that much because you already knew that you would have to work late on occasion.

If the disruption is major—perhaps you find out that your job requires you to pull all-nighters three or four nights a week—it invalidates your expectations. You may experience confusion, fear, anxiety, anger, and a loss of emotional equilibrium. When major disruptions occur in the workplace, these symptoms can produce disabling consequences for both individuals and organizations.

As I said earlier, humans are the most control-oriented animals on the planet. The methods different people use to meet their control needs vary greatly and are at times not easily observed. Some people are obviously trying to rule their own destinies (e.g., a body builder sculpting his or her physique). But often we express our needs for self-regulation more subtly. For example, learning to use a new software package designed to enhance productivity or the decision to file for divorce are both forms of attempting to control or at least influence one's future.

Given the magnitude of change taking place at the personal, organizational, and societal levels of our lives, it has become difficult, to say the least, to live an orderly, predictable existence. For this reason, our ability to influence our environment holds more than a little importance.

When we are unable to meet our control needs, we become disoriented. When we can meet these needs, we gain a feeling of stability and psychological comfort so powerful that attaining this state is one of the most potent motivators of human behavior. Over the next twenty-four hours, pay attention to how much of your time and energy is dedicated to learning:

- *what has happened* after events took place that were meaningful to you ("What did we do to make the customers so mad?" "Why did the teacher keep you after school?");
- *what is happening* ("Can you explain to us what you are doing as you go through the procedure?" "Do you still love me?"); and
- *what will happen* ("With the reduced interest rate, we should expect an increase in business by next quarter," "Let's use the sonogram so that we will know whether to paint the nursery blue or pink").

You will find that you devote a great deal of your life to gaining enough information to understand and try to control (or at least influence) your environment.

When current reality differs only slightly from what we expected, we believe that we are able to accurately predict events and prepare for them. Even when the events themselves are negative and unavoidable, we can achieve a form of psychological equilibrium by not being surprised that they are happening.

Regardless of how conscious or unconscious the effort, when you gain a sense of control over your life, it stems from your ability to match expectations with perceived reality. This match or mismatch triggers the human emotions of comfort or dismay. That is why the key difference between equilibrium and chaos is not the volume, momentum, and complexity of the surrounding events, but the degree to which one's expectations are met.

Some of the most frightening situations are those in which we not only lack a sense of control over our environment, but we are shocked that this lack of control could occur—again, we are surprised that we are surprised.

WHAT TO CONTROL

People seem to have a preference regarding what they would like to control. The whole universe would be nice, but most of us will settle for at least controlling the events that affect us personally—if not these events, then the people involved in these events.

If this is not possible and we must endure others doing as they please, then it is crucial that we are able to govern our own actions. When we are surprised by our own behavior, it is essential that we—at the very least—preside over the emotions that well up within us.

If this succession of events cannot be controlled and our needs are left unfulfilled, we find ourselves thrown into a state of disequilibrium that becomes progressively more uncomfortable to endure. Nevertheless, we are resourceful animals; so when any of these levels of control cannot be met directly, we negotiate with ourselves to accept indirect control as a secondary source of comfort. We do this by seeking solace gained by acknowledging that full control is not possible. Even with negative events we can't directly control, anticipating them meets our unconscious need for predictability to some extent.

The gift of anticipation is both a blessing and a curse. It can help us ready ourselves for events, or it can be a final blow. Without the ability to anticipate, we lose our last chance for even indirect control. If anticipation is inoperative, we are defenseless against the devastating impact of future shock. Being surprised that we are surprised is at the heart of feeling that the world around us is transforming faster than our own speed of change can accommodate.

MAJOR CHANGE IS LOSS OF CONTROL

Figure 2 represents a summary of the powerful influence control has on how people perceive and react to change. Three important implications can be drawn from this chart:

1. Change is considered major when it is *perceived* to be so by those affected.
2. Major change is the result of significant disruption in established expectations.
3. Major change occurs when people believe they have lost control over some important aspect of their lives or their environment.

KNOWING YOUR ASSIMILATION CAPACITY

Assimilation is the process we use to adjust to the positive or negative implications of a major shift in our expectations. Assimilating, or absorbing, such change is costly, because it requires resources to make the shift. The high price of assimilation includes reduced intellectual energy, increased psychological stress, and diminished physical stamina and health.

Every person, group, and organization has a certain number

THE HUMAN REACTION TO CHANGE

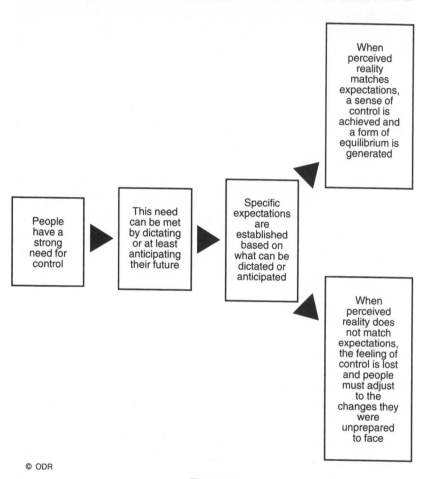

© ODR

Figure 2

of assimilation points available. These points represent our capacity to absorb change. No one has an infinite supply of assimilation points. But resilient people have learned how to increase the number of their assimilation points and how to stay within their personal assimilation budget.

Imagine that you have six hundred assimilation points to pay for absorbing all the changes that will take place in your life over the next year. The six hundred points and twelve months are arbitrary, hypothetical figures chosen purely for discussion purposes. The number of assimilation points that you pay for a given change depends on the degree to which that change matches what you expect. For example, say you have the responsibility of speaking in front of your management team once each month. If you arrive in the morning before you are supposed to talk and find out that there will be three or four other staff members in the audience, it may cost you an assimilation point or two, but it won't be a significant drain. Much more expensive in terms of assimilation points would be coming in to find out that you had to speak in front of the entire company. Both major and minor changes cost assimilation points, but adjusting to the minor disruption of a few extra audience members would be far less expensive than dealing with the major disruption of talking in front of a radically larger and more intimidating group.

THE COST OF DISRUPTION

Disruptive change always exacts an assimilation fee. We spend assimilation points whether we accept or reject changes that come our way.

We consume assimilation points whether we initiate change or others thrust it upon us. Conventional logic dictates that if a change is your idea or you contributed to it in some way, you will probably not resist it. So the common belief is that no assimilation costs are associated with our own change initiatives. But our research contradicts this contention. Some of the strongest resistance occurs when we get exactly what we asked for—if what we asked for causes a significant departure from our expectations.

Examples: selling one's home and buying a bigger one, securing approval for a reorganization plan, or winning a military victory. Changes like these can catch people unaware because they did not expect them to bear much of a negative cost. The likely response is: "Since it was my idea and I got what I wanted, how could it take a toll on me?"

The assimilation process involves reacting to both the cause of a change and its short- and long-term implications. The things actually being changed usually drain the least from assimilation resources. It is the unanticipated implications of change that usually devastate us.

For example, we have found that most companies with a poor track record for implementing new technology focus too much on the hardware and software. Organizations that successfully introduce new technology concern themselves with the *implications* of the new system as much or more so than with the technology itself.

A case in point: The widespread introduction of personal computers has dramatically altered our expectations of work performance. When a boss provides one of her staff with a PC and spreadsheet software, one implication may be that she now expects that person to produce ten times the volume of financial analysis previously possible. Also, instead of sitting around a table sharing information and talking with coworkers, the staff person is now confined to a small cubicle and the glare of what he perceives to be an impersonal piece of hardware. The worker's expectations for a typical workday have undergone a major change.

What does the worker complain about in such a case? He's likely to curse the new computer. So the company spends money for more computer training or buys the worker an expanded system. Yet the worker remains in the same cubicle with the same perceived problems as before.

The true problems lie underneath the surface of the hardware and software complaints. What lurks below are the real issues of "peopleware":

- Maybe he's not a great financial whiz, but he has been a master of synthesizing many people's input into something greater than the sum of its parts. Now he's reduced to boring, repetitive number crunching, which was never his forte.
- He's suffering from the cutoff of social interaction. In the good old days, discussions of the latest political issues or sports offered relief from the tedious nature of the financial work.
- He may have never learned to type in school. Suddenly, the brilliant guy around the office is embarrassed when his coworkers watch his clumsy hunt-and-peck typing.

Ironically, even computer professionals resist change associated with computerization. For example, I have been working with a group of Ernst & Young consultants that help organizations automate the software development process. They have found that even though the clients' computer programmers and analysts may have devoted their entire careers to computerizing business functions, they often react extremely negatively to the computerization of their own functions!

In nearly every project plagued by resistance to the change itself, there is an underlying, negative personal implication for one or more people affected by the change. These hidden implications cause most of the assimilation problems.

To have a solid foundation for the information in the rest of this chapter, let's review what we have already discussed regarding the dynamics of change. Change occurs when people view their challenges to be greater than their capabilities or vice versa. Change is perceived to be positive when you feel in control by being able to accurately anticipate events and influence your immediate environment (or at least prepare for the consequences). Resistance to major change will occur regardless of whether the event is initially perceived as positive or negative and without regard to whether it is self-initiated or brought on by others.

And, finally, assimilating the short- and long-term implications of change is usually more costly than adjusting to the change itself.

THE PARADOX

Another key aspect to the nature of change is how we use up our assimilation points. The demands on our assimilation capacity come from more than one direction:

- *Micro changes* affect you, your spouse, family, or close friends and associates.
- *Organizational changes* occur not just at work but with any institution that affects your life, such as your church or synagogue, professional association, or union.
- *Macro changes* affect you as part of a large constituency. The global implications of third world debt and progress in reducing racial tension in South Africa are events that have macro implications.

Micro change is when "I" must change; organizational change is when "we" must change; macro change is when "everyone" must change.

Paradoxically, even though the term *macro change* sounds big, it actually has the least effect on an individual's day-to-day behavior. Macro changes such as environmental pollution or increasing crime seem so far removed from us that they appear not to be tangible.

Only when changes affect us personally do we begin to sit up and take notice. The Persian Gulf War was an event with only macro implications—unless you had a friend or relative among the troops. Then it became a micro issue as well, and your consumption of assimilation resources shot up.

Suppose you have a routine that includes listening to the news every morning while dressing for work. As you listen, you take in all kinds of information about political, economic, and environmental turmoil: a new scandal involving a major political figure, medical waste washing up on the beach. You hear that another fifty thousand acres of rain forest in Brazil have burned, the economy is shifting again, there has been another oil spill, and biologists may have just discovered something about our DNA that fundamentally redefines the way we conceive of aging and disease. Despite the large-scale importance of these news accounts, you are through thinking about them by the time you finish getting ready for work. It's not that you didn't pay attention, but the issues are so big and seem so far away. Unconsciously, you say to yourself, "I am just one person. What am I going to do about these things? I can't make a difference." Not many assimilation points are used here.

When you arrive at work, you learn that your boss has decided to install a new organizational structure that is going to completely destroy the power base you have been building for the past ten years; this grabs your attention, causing you to expend a lot of assimilation points. You go home that night to find that your kid is in a drug-rehabilitation clinic, and your mother-in-law just moved in. These events present you with even more serious assimilation problems and a severe drain on your remaining assimilation points. Thus, micro change demands first priority.

There is an interesting paradox about the way people relate to change: Even though we witness macro issues like technological breakthroughs, wars, and ecological disasters, the single biggest change for most people would be the moving in of their mother-in-law. The important lesson here is that if you consider yourself an architect of change—whether it is organizational (the installation of new information systems) or macro (a new worldwide economic order)—the intended goals will not be achieved unless there are micro implications for the people involved.

Until people see a personal connection between their own behavior and resolution of the organizational or macro issue, the problem is simply an intellectual exercise and not personally relevant:

"Boss, I couldn't agree with you more about the need for quality improvement around here. Let me know if I can help you get the others to do their part."

"I am appalled at the federal deficit. We've got to do something; but don't increase my taxes and don't take away the social programs I support."

Much of our problem with making organizational or macro changes is that we fail to adequately communicate to people the impact these decisions will have on them personally. No wonder these kinds of changes are so difficult to enact.

OVERLAPPING IMPACT

The dysfunctional behavior associated with future shock is not usually due to a single change event. It more typically occurs from the affects of multiple, overlapping changes.

Let's go back to the hypothetical reserve of six hundred assimilation points that we discussed earlier and build a picture of how they could be consumed during the year (see Figure 3). Some of the points, but not many of them, will be used to absorb the implications of large social issues—macro changes like world hunger, nuclear waste, and environmental pollution. One of the reasons problems like these never seem to go away is that we cannot sustain our interest and investment in them. They just seem too distant.

You will use a greater portion of your points assimilating organizational change. Assimilation problems often happen when an organization incrementalizes its change projects. This means that one group within your organization is told to plan an acquisition, another one to introduce new technology, and yet another group to focus on a new "total quality" initiative.

These groups are charged with developing an implementation strategy for their project. Each is confident about its particular plan's demand on assimilation points because, as they see it:

FUTURE SHOCK USUALLY OCCURS
BECAUSE OF THE AGGREGATE
IMPACT OF SEVERAL CHANGES

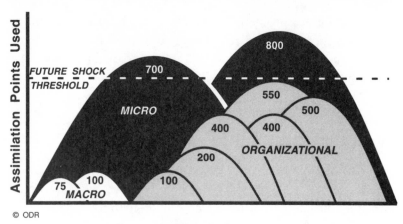

© ODR

Figure 3

"Our project is in good shape. Everyone has six hundred points, and our plan only costs four hundred." Of course, the other groups are having similar discussions and making similar demands.

The problem is that management doesn't collect the proper information to develop a complete picture of what is about to happen. They fail to realize that all these changes are going to affect the same constituencies within the organization. Given this incremental approach, it is easy to see how you will surpass your six-hundred-point threshold and fall victim to future shock.

Now let's examine what happens back at your home with the micro level of change. This is where your greatest expenditure of the points occurs due to your child's drug problem and your mother-in-law. Because of these difficulties you are running low on assimilation points even before you get to work.

In fact, a disturbing comment we hear more and more from people is that they sometimes go to work to rest. "I'll trade my problems at home any day for the relatively minor hassles at the office."

I want to caution you here about the trap into which many people fall when introducing change. If you haven't built a comprehensive picture of the total assimilation drain on the people affected by multiple changes, you may be seduced into thinking that a particular project will be assimilated without much of a problem.

Whether you introduce a new process into an organization or inform your spouse that you won't be home for dinner, it can be shocking to initiate what appears to be a little change only to face a tremendous amount of resistance. If the people involved are already experiencing an assimilation deficit, your little fifty-, seventy-five-, or hundred-point change that should not have been difficult to deal with can cause trauma.

Remember, people do not have three different point allocations. They don't have six hundred each for the company, for home, and for large-scale events. They have six hundred points total. Assimilation points are like time and money; you never seem to have enough.

There is a tremendous amount of competition for the points necessary to introduce change successfully. Most of these points are consumed by family issues and personal problems, while a few are also apportioned for the macro changes that everyone faces.

Competition for the limited assimilation points also exists within a single organization. To introduce change in a naïve fashion—assuming that assimilation is not costing a great deal or that there are plenty of points available—is to ask for a serious case of future shock.

People who manage change well know intuitively that once they are nearing the future-shock threshold with the people in their organization, they can no longer just announce change— they must orchestrate it. They would never issue a memo saying,

"We need for every division to reduce its head count by 15 percent during the next three months. Are there any questions?" They know that this kind of behavior leads to dysfunctional reactions. Instead, they approach change as a complex-but-manageable process, one that requires careful planning and tough prioritizing to avoid exceeding the future-shock threshold.

The capacity to absorb a great deal of change is directly related to the number of assimilation points available to a person or group and the number expended during the implementation process. Resilient people have more available points and use fewer of them, thereby conserving their assimilation resources for future changes.

We have learned that neither the amount of money a change costs nor whether it is desired is a good indicator of how people will respond to change. A much more reliable indicator is how surprised by a change people are. Major change occurs when expectations about important events or issues are *significantly disrupted*—when people anticipate one thing is going to happen, and yet something drastically different occurs.

The resulting stress generates the disabling consequences of future shock for individuals, organizations, or entire countries. Improving the resilience of people involved in change guards against future shock. This, as we'll discuss later, is done by increasing the number of assimilation points that they have available and minimizing the number of points expended on any one change.

THE FIVE KEY PRINCIPLES IN THE "NATURE OF CHANGE" PATTERN

When involved in major organizational change, you can enhance resilience if you:

1. Realize that control is what we all seek in our lives, and the ambiguity caused by the disruption of expectations is what we all fear and avoid.

2. Are able to exercise some degree of direct or indirect control over what happens during the implementation of change.
3. Can assimilate change at a speed commensurate with the pace of the events taking place around you.
4. Understand the micro implications of organizational or macro change.
5. Face a total assimilation demand from the micro, organizational, and macro transitions in your life that is within your absorption limits.

CHAPTER 6

THE PROCESS OF CHANGE

*T*he second support pattern, the *process of change,* outlines the mechanisms of human transitions. The way we relate to change in our lives reveals a great deal about why some of us succeed and some of us fail at sustaining major change. Those of us who view change as something that either happens or doesn't happen seem to be particularly vulnerable to future shock. Conversely, those who have the fewest problems during change appear to be protected to some extent by the fact that they approach it as an ongoing process.

People who adapt more slowly than the pace of the changes occurring around them do so partly because they have a low tolerance for ambiguity and therefore they generally perceive life in binary terms: yes or no, black or white. Managers like this do not see a merger or the introduction of new technology as an ongoing endeavor that needs constant attention. Instead, they view change projects as events that have a distinct before and after, as onetime shots that either fire or fizzle: "The merger is complete because the senior executives have reached agreement." "The new software was delivered yesterday; we're ready to go."

In the age of the sound bite and ready-aim-fire mentalities, this view of change as having an on/off button has become common. The media deal with events that they can report and analyze as isolated happenings rather than as unfolding history. When people take this approach at face value, they begin to believe that, overnight, governments are toppled, systems are scrapped, and wars are won. "The papers are signed; it's a done deal."

Resilient people tend to avoid the more limited binary view of change. They realize that major change is a fluid phenomenon, like an ice cube melting and refreezing. In the status-quo phase, the ice cube is relatively fixed, frozen. But the "pain"—the cost of unresolved problems or missed opportunities—causes the status quo to heat up, forcing it to flow into a transitional phase. Finally, when the process reaches the desired state, change refreezes and solidifies to form into a new status quo.

In today's fast-paced world, refreezing to a permanent state is not likely. Most of our time will be spent in transitions, not stable states. To understand how we live in a constant state of "in between," we must view transitions as consisting of periods of "leaving from" something, periods of reordering or reconstruction, and periods of "going to" something—even if the goals to which we are heading are constantly moving.

THE THREE PHASES OF CHANGE

A model first developed by social psychologist Kurt Lewin* in 1958 classifies the change process into three phases: the present state, the transition state, and the desired state. The present state

---

* Lewin, Kurt. "Group Decision and Social Change," in *Readings in Social Psychology,* ed. E. E. Maccoby, T. M. Newcomb, and E. L. Hartley (New York: Holt, Rinehart and Winston, 1958), pp. 197–211.

is the status quo—an established equilibrium that continues indefinitely until a force disrupts it (see Figure 4).

The transition state is the phase during which we disengage from the status quo. During this period, we develop new attitudes or behaviors that lead to the desired state. To attain what we want (the desired state), we must pass through the uncertain, uncomfortable phase of the transition state.

Keeping major change alive is only possible when the pain of the present state exceeds the cost of the transition state. It would be expensive to leave behind your house and possessions during a flood, but the likelihood that you would drown by staying makes abandoning your home the least costly course of action. Likewise, it would be risky to leave a safe, secure job. But if a new position at twice the salary was offered to you, the pain of missing the opportunity could be too great to pass up.

No one likes existing in a state of limbo because the in-between periods in our lives are filled with instability, conflict, and high stress. This volatile phase of the change process occurs when the equilibrium of the present state has been disrupted, but the stability of the desired state is yet to be attained. For example, when a person is first divorced, he or she will often continue to

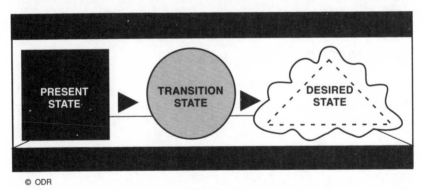

© ODR

Figure 4

feel emotionally attached to the former spouse even after the papers are signed. During the transition state, people are neither what they were, nor are they yet what they will become.

Because of the nebulous and often chaotic nature of this phase, people will often attempt to regain their equilibrium by reverting back to the way things were. Many change projects are never completed because the people involved could not tolerate the sense of ambiguity and lack of control inherent to the transition phase.

Despite the sometimes intense discomfort of uncertainty, there are circumstances in which people will engage the unknown. As the leaders of the emerging democracies of Eastern Europe are discovering, change toward free-market economics may be disruptive, frightening, and expensive, but they have no choice. The price of *not* changing—economic stagnation, isolation from the European community—is unacceptably high. For these nations, change is not just a good idea—it's an imperative.

I cannot overstate how frightening it is to lose a sense of control or influence. People will even choose to stay in familiar situations that they know are not working rather than face the ambiguity of the unknown. Many times, a battered wife will remain for years, even a lifetime, with a physically violent husband. Women have reported that, among other reasons, they have stayed with brutal husbands because breaking out of the relationship was even more frightening than the beatings. Even though the situation may be physically and emotionally abusive, such women have at least learned what to expect, and there is an odd comfort in being able to anticipate the future—even a negative future.

Before you discount the "battered-wife syndrome" as an unusual predicament that doesn't reflect your situation, ask yourself when you last stayed in a bad situation longer than you should have (e.g., a negative relationship, poor technology, a weak organizational plan). For most of us, the unknown is so terrifying that we will remain with what we have long after it is apparent that it is punishing to do so.

The tension caused by a status quo that is no longer worth the price it takes to maintain it necessitates a new operating framework. For the resilient, this holds the promise of opportunity. Eagerness to reduce the stress and anxiety of transitional ambiguity generally makes us more receptive to attaining the goals of the change. We seek out information that will help us create a new stable state. Learning is the foremost opportunity stemming from change.

As I said, the difficulty of the transition state forces some people to abort the process shortly after initiating it; only by developing the resolve to sustain the transition can you attain the desired state.

SURVIVAL OF THE FITTEST

Charles Darwin first taught us that there have always been far more losers than winners. More members of a species expire than survive; it's simply natural law. Similarly, there are many more organizations that initiate change than those that can successfully sustain it.

By winners, I am referring to those resilient individuals or organizations who manage change at a speed that allows them to effectively implement the human and technical aspects of transition on time and within budget. Losers are those individuals or organizations who bring change projects in significantly late or over budget or who settle for changes less substantive than those needed to remain competitive.

Winners are able to achieve the full benefit of their change initiatives. Losers are victims of change who either never achieve their initiatives or, if they do, it's only after expending a great deal more time and money than they had anticipated.

One of the key differences between winners and losers is the tenacity winners demonstrate. Losers tend to announce projects only to see them falter and abandoned at a later date. What this indicates is that even losers can *initiate* major change. Issuing a memo or making an announcement of a change project is not the same thing as ensuring its success.

Over the years, I have heard losers give many reasons for announcing their changes: "Our competitors are doing it"; "Everybody at last year's convention was talking about it"; "We didn't think we had much to risk by trying it"; or, my all-time favorite, "We read about it in *The Wall Street Journal,* and it seemed like a good idea at the time."

After observing winners in many different settings, I have learned that there is only one circumstance that motivates them to make and sustain a major change: when they can no longer afford the status quo. It requires no special skill to just announce that a change is going to take place—losers do it every day. Winners, on the other hand, understand that when the price for maintaining the status quo is higher than the price of transition, making a change is mandatory.

Hence, winners are selective about the changes that they undertake; many have a certain intuition for determining when a change project warrants special care and planning. Winners also believe that some problems and opportunities are simply not worth the investment that addressing them in a structured, disciplined manner would require. After completing a cost-benefit analysis, a winner might determine that updating the company's existing technology carries a price tag greater than its worth. Whereas losers tend to make change look cheap and easy, winners keep firmly in mind Murphy's dictum that if something can go wrong, it will, and thus everything is harder than it looks.

Major organizational change is too disruptive, time consuming, and expensive to approach lightly. Managers can justify the risk and resources of attempting significant change only if they feel that their part of the organization will slip competitively or miss critical opportunities unless the change goals are achieved. Engaging minor change has no such restrictions, but you should not undertake major change unless the organization cannot afford to fail at the implementation.

A BURNING PLATFORM

For years, I had difficulty finding a way to convey the level of resolve that I observed winners display during change. Then one day, I watched a television news interview that said it all.

At nine-thirty on a July evening in 1988, a disastrous explosion and fire occurred on an oil-drilling platform in the North Sea off the coast of Scotland. One hundred and sixty-six crew members and two rescuers lost their lives in the worst catastrophe in the twenty-five-year history of North Sea oil exploration. One of the sixty-three crew members who survived was a superintendent on the rig, Andy Mochan. His interview helped me find a way to describe the resolve that change winners manifest.

From his hospital bed, he told of being awakened by the explosion and alarms. He said that he ran from his quarters to the platform edge and jumped fifteen stories from the platform to the water. Because of the water's temperature, he knew that he could live a maximum of only twenty minutes if he were not rescued. Also, oil had surfaced and ignited. Yet Andy jumped 150 feet in the middle of the night into an ocean of burning oil and debris.

When asked why he took that potentially fatal leap, he did not hesitate. He said, "It was either jump or fry." He chose possible death over certain death. Consider this:

- He didn't jump because he felt confident that he would survive.
- He didn't jump because it seemed like a good idea.
- He didn't jump because he thought it would be intellectually intriguing.
- He didn't jump because it was a personal growth experience.

He jumped because he had no choice—the price of staying on the platform, of maintaining the status quo, was too high. This is the same type of situation in which many business, social, and political leaders find themselves every day. We sometimes *have* to make some changes, no matter how uncertain and frightening they are. We, like Andy Mochan, would face a price too high for not doing so.

An organizational burning platform exists when maintaining the status quo becomes prohibitively expensive. Major change is always costly, but when the present course of action is even more expensive, a burning-platform situation erupts.

The key characteristic that distinguishes a decision made in a burning-platform situation from all other decisions is not the degree of reason or emotion involved, but the *level of resolve*. When an organization is on a burning platform, the decision to make a major change is not just a good idea—it is a business imperative.

THE FORCE BEHIND THE URGENCY

The urgency of burning-platform situations motivates us to sustain major change. Two types of situations can generate this urgency: the high price of unresolved problems or the high cost of missed opportunities.

Figures 5 and 6 provide typical examples of the price of unresolved problems or missed opportunities. The examples at the lower end of each scale represent "good ideas." As you move up the scale, the costs shift to those that are too expensive to pay. These situations that arise are burning platforms—business imperatives. The line between a good idea and a business imperative is subjective; each organization must define this distinction for itself.

Most organizations jeopardize their ability to sustain imperative changes because they embark on too many good ideas—changes that they want to do, are justified in doing, ones that will produce benefits and may be popular with the employees, but are not imperatives. To conserve assimilation resources, it is vital that organizations focus their attention on burning platform–type situations.

THE PRICE FOR FAILING TO TAKE ADVANTAGE OF AN OPPORTUNITY

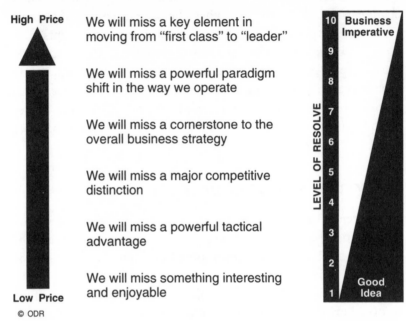

High Price

We will miss a key element in moving from "first class" to "leader"

We will miss a powerful paradigm shift in the way we operate

We will miss a cornerstone to the overall business strategy

We will miss a major competitive distinction

We will miss a powerful tactical advantage

We will miss something interesting and enjoyable

Low Price

© ODR

LEVEL OF RESOLVE

10 — Business Imperative
9
8
7
6
5
4
3
2
1 — Good Idea

Figure 5

TIMING IS EVERYTHING

The resolve to change that organizations develop during burning-platform circumstances can surface early or late in the game. When the resolve forms early, the company has anticipated what the price or pain of the status quo will be if the desired action is not taken. When the resolve develops late, the company is already paying a price for the status quo that is too expensive to bear.

"Current pain" is what inspires commitment to change late in a situation. Unfortunately, only short-term tactical action is possible at that point. When the resolve to change comes early,

THE PRICE FOR FAILING TO SOLVE A PROBLEM

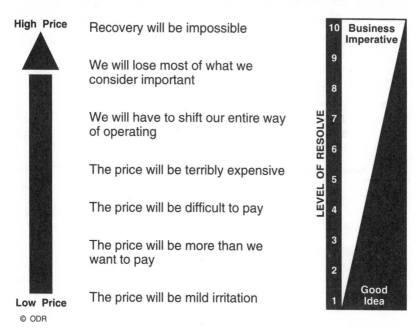

High Price

Recovery will be impossible

We will lose most of what we consider important

We will have to shift our entire way of operating

The price will be terribly expensive

The price will be difficult to pay

The price will be more than we want to pay

The price will be mild irritation

Low Price

© ODR

LEVEL OF RESOLVE

10 Business Imperative
9
8
7
6
5
4
3
2
1 Good Idea

Figure 6

it is due to "anticipated pain." Anticipated pain can be more powerful due to the extra time available in which to make strategic moves; however, it is often more difficult to convince people to take direct action when no current pain is felt.

Commitment to change can develop during either the anticipated or current time frames. If the commitment to act forms too early, it won't be sustained; if it develops too late, it won't matter.

If a burning-platform situation is at hand, the issue is not *will* the necessary commitment to act be generated, but *when*. If change is truly imperative, commitment is inevitable; in these situations, the crucial variable is the timing of the resolve.

HOW PAIN DRIVES CHANGE

	PROBLEM	OPPORTUNITY
CURRENT	SITUATION: "We're in trouble now." PAIN: The immediate loss of our market dominance, job security, organizational survival, etc.	SITUATION: "If we act immediately, we can take advantage of this situation." PAIN: The loss of a potential advantage that is within our grasp.
ANTICIPATED	SITUATION: "We're going to be in trouble." PAIN: The impending loss of our market dominance, job security, organizational survival, etc.	SITUATION: "In the future, we could be in a position to profit from what is going to happen." PAIN: The loss of a potential advantage that is possible to achieve in the future.

© ODR

Figure 7

I first became aware of the importance of the timing of commitment many years ago while counseling a patient dying of alcohol-related problems. The night he died, I held his hand as he pleaded for God to grant him more time to resolve his life's struggles, which he was now confident that he could overcome. I realized at that moment—as he begged for another chance—that you could not ask for any more commitment than he demonstrated. He was sincere, honest, and intense. In all likelihood, what he was feeling constituted the exact level of resolve necessary for him to have maintained his recovery from alcoholism. But it was too late.

He truly was committed to stop drinking—the problem was that by then his liver was beyond repair. If your organization is facing a burning-platform situation, don't worry about generating commitment; worry about timing this commitment so that it can make a difference before irreversible damage is done.

In today's irregular business environment, more and more organizations are finding themselves on burning platforms. Leaders are facing a status quo that they can no longer afford. Although transition may be disruptive and expensive, organizations feeling the heat understand that they have no choice but to change.

Change is not always necessitated by existing or anticipated *problems*; sometimes, emerging *opportunities* require major transitions. The urgency of burning platforms may result from either positive or negative circumstances, or it may stem from a visionary's drive for excellence. Regardless, the common denominator for all burning-platform situations is urgency, necessity—*resolve*.

TWO PREREQUISITES FOR MAJOR ORGANIZATIONAL CHANGE

Let's revisit the process of change that we discussed earlier. This time, we will look for the figure to depict two prerequisites for successful organizational change:

1. *Pain:* a critical mass of information that justifies breaking from the status quo.
2. *Remedy:* desirable, accessible actions that would solve the problem or take advantage of the opportunity afforded by the current situation.

Pain management provides the motivation to pull away from the present; remedy selling provides the motivation to proceed to the desired state. Every successful transition from the present state to the desired state entails these two prerequisites.

For prolonged change, both elements must work together.

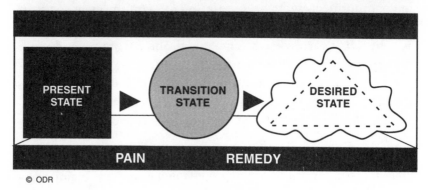

CHANGE IS A PROCESS

PRESENT STATE

TRANSITION STATE

DESIRED STATE

PAIN   REMEDY

© ODR

Figure 8

But losers initiate change with only an attractive remedy to provide the motivation. Remedies without a costly status quo produce short-term interests which often dwindle. And, of course, pain without remedy produces only ulcers, not change.

NO PAIN, NO GAIN

The success of a change project depends equally on pain management and remedy selling. We will focus on pain management here, not because it is more important than remedy selling, but because organizations usually neglect it.

Change-related pain is the level of discomfort that we experience when we can't meet our goals (current pain) or don't expect to meet them (anticipated pain). This discomfort stems from either the unresolved problems or missed opportunities of the status quo. **Orchestrating pain messages throughout an institution is the first step in developing organizational commitment to change.** The goal of pain management is to motivate people to pull away from what they are doing now and develop a strong commitment to making a change. To accomplish this you must manage information in such a way that it generates the necessary incentive for discontinuing the status quo.

How much pain people are willing to endure before they shift from the present state to the desired state and their actual level of attraction to the desired state depends on each individual's *frame of reference*. A person's frame of reference is his or her unconscious model for making sense of the world.

Frames of reference exert a powerful influence on our lives, functioning as a sort of closed-loop system. Our frames of reference determine our expectations, which influence what we perceive and how we process information. The information we process drives what we think, which is how we establish the alternatives that we believe are available for making decisions. We engage in actions based on these decisions that, in turn, usually reinforce our original expectations. This self-perpetuating system is often a major source of resistance because many people unconsciously think, "I'll believe it when I see it, and I'll see it when I believe it."

THE WOLF IN THE CLOSET

An example of how frames of reference influence the way people approach change can be found in a comparison of the banking and computer industries. In many cases, managing pain in the traditionally conservative banking business has required more effort than it does in other industries.

For instance, it is not uncommon for computer-industry executives to believe that rapid, effective change is essential to survival. Because it is part of their frame of reference to expect and easily acclimate to swift transition, they have little allegiance to the status quo. Conversely, bankers have historically perceived change as "risky," and, until recent years (before deregulation), their loyalty to the way that they have always operated was extremely strong. Bankers traditionally perceived the price of change as more expensive than the cost of maintaining the status quo.

Comparing different frames of reference within the same company also sheds light on varying perceptions of change. A top corporate executive who is surprised by negative reactions to a change project within her company may not have regarded the project as a major transition. The change may have only slightly altered operations from her standpoint. In other words, from her frame of reference, the change was a minor one. Regardless of the executive's perception of the project, further down the chain of command some poor cog in the machine is spinning like crazy, unprepared to handle the speed at which his world now turns.

THE ESCALATING SPIN OF CHANGE

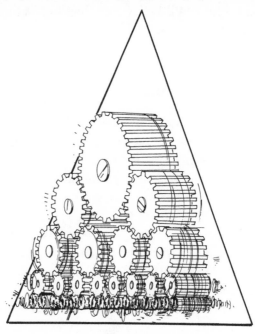

© ODR

Figure 9

To manage this sort of difference in perception, leaders must recognize the distinction between their world and that of those lower in the organization. Managing effective transitions does not allow for dealing with a single reality; it involves managing multiple realities as seen through various people's fears, hopes, and aspirations—their frames of reference.

Leaders who successfully promote resilience during change make decisions in light of how people at all levels will interpret their actions. **Even if a new initiative is absorbed easily by senior management but causes significant disruption for others,** *winners* **approach the task as if it is a major change for those who perceive it that way.**

A lesson on how to manage perceptions to ease the assimilation of change can be found in the way Thomas Edison introduced the electric light bulb in 1879. Edison perceived that there would be a negative initial reaction to his device simply because it was so foreign to most people's frame of reference. To dampen the shock of his radical innovation, he designed the new lights to resemble as closely as possible the gas lights of the period.

Edison's attention to detail was remarkable. Rather than installing fixtures in the ceiling where they would cast light most efficiently, he placed them on the walls in the standard gas-light fixtures. He even shaped the bulbs themselves to resemble gas light in appearance and intensity. Although the wall attachments required more difficult wiring, he regarded the extra effort as more than worth it.

When people first saw Edison's display, they detected little that was different from what they were accustomed to. They easily assimilated the change because Edison had tailored this revolutionary device to fit their frames of reference. Edison knew that human perception is often the biggest hurdle to implementing change.

A personal story may further illuminate the importance of managing perceptions. When my youngest son, Chase, was four years old, he watched a movie one night that frightened him. For the next several months, he was convinced that at night when he was alone in his room there was a wolf in his closet. All the explanation and conclusive evidence in the world could not convince him that there wasn't a wolf waiting to pounce on him once it was dark.

My wife and I turned on the lights, we went through the closet item by item, and we sealed off the closet doors. Nothing mattered. He was sure that there was a wolf in the closet waiting to attack. No matter how often we invoked the adult reality of the situation, we could not change his perception that the wolf existed.

If we had attempted to manage Chase's fear the way most managers deal with the concerns of those affected by change, the only thing that we would have taught him was that we don't know what we're talking about. The typical approach is to say, "Look, there can't possibly be a wolf in the closet. I'm the dad, and dads know these things."

We resolved the situation by appealing to Chase's perceptions, tackling the problem within his frame of reference—not ours. Chase's godmother bought him a large paper-mâché figure of Michelangelo (one of the Teenage Mutant Ninja Turtles, of course, not the Renaissance painter and sculptor). With the Ninja Turtle safely guarding the closet, Chase no longer had to worry about the wolf. Any four-year-old knows that there isn't a wolf on the prowl that is a match for Michelangelo.

Managing perceptions of change in a work situation should be handled no differently. You have to acknowledge that for the people in your organization, the "wolf in the closet" does exist.

Treating Chase as stupid or ridiculous for believing in the wolf would not have solved the problem. Telling him to stop crying would have only diminished the visible symptoms. Similarly, managers can sometimes remove observable *symptoms* of resistance with threats, insults, or by good-natured cajoling. But the underlying problem will not go away and, worst of all, the resistance will go underground where you can't detect it. By treating workers as if their fears and anxieties about change are so much "unnecessary crying," you are inviting them to keep their concerns to themselves. And that is dangerous for both you and them.

Change management is perception management. Superficial, patronizing responses are never a substitute for letting employees know that you understand and care about their concerns—at their level. To gain commitment to move from the present state to the desired state, managers must be willing to honor (with action) employee perceptions of reality. But you don't necessarily have to agree with them to show that you understand their feelings. I did not have to agree with Chase that there was a wolf in his closet to understand how frightened I might feel if I were four and I had seen that movie.

In summary, winners enhance their resilience in part by approaching change as an understandable process with phases that can be anticipated and managed. They view change as an unfolding continuum and demonstrate a high tolerance for its ambiguity. They plan and execute movement architecturally from the present state through a transition phase to the desired goal. And their plans include pain-management strategies to help people disengage from the status quo as well as desirable and accessible remedies to attract them to the desired change.

Change-related pain is the level of discomfort a person experiences when his or her goals are not being met (current pain) or are not expected to be met (anticipated pain) due to the circumstances of the status quo. Managing these pain messages is the first step in developing commitment to change. The goal of pain management is to cause a shift from the existing status quo and build and sustain commitment to the change. You must develop a critical mass of information and then orchestrate it to motivate a discontinuation of the status quo. How much pain a person is willing to endure before he or she shifts from the present state and what it may take to attract a person to the desired state varies from person to person.

THE SIX KEY PRINCIPLES IN
THE "PROCESS OF CHANGE" PATTERN

When involved in major organizational change, you can enhance resilience if you:

1. Approach change as an unfolding process rather than a binary (either/or) event.
2. Accept that you will either pay for getting what you want or you will pay for not getting what you want and the payments may come early or late—but change is expensive, and you *will* pay.
3. Believe the status quo is far more expensive than the cost of transition.
4. Accept the discomfort of ambiguity as a natural reaction to transition.
5. Are attracted to remedies you see as accessible.
6. Are presented with changes in a manner that takes into account your frame of reference.

CHAPTER 7

THE ROLES OF CHANGE

Wouldn't it be wonderful if you could consult your organizational chart to determine quickly who would play the key roles in a change project? Regrettably, the volatility of major change makes this method rarely, if ever, successful. The third support pattern focuses on the *roles of change* and their importance to the change process.

Role assignments for change projects seldom follow a linear path through an organization. Working relationships can be highly complex and convoluted, with people often playing more than one role and frequently shifting roles once a change is under way. For example, say you are a line worker in an auto plant. Obviously, your supervisor is your boss in most situations, and you look to him to legitimize important changes before you act. But when a labor-management dispute causes the union to call a strike, it is your union shop steward who has the sanctioning power to get you to walk off the job. In this case, your supervisor has little influence when it comes to whether or not you participate in the strike.

Resilient people demonstrate an understanding of the key roles that operate during change and adapt to the varying configurations. People who lack resilience have difficulty keeping up with who is playing what role and, therefore, they usually fail at change. Winners recognize that orchestrating role assignments is essential to successful transition.

There are four distinct roles critical to the change process: sponsors, agents, targets, and advocates.

Sponsors

A sponsor is the individual or group who has the power to sanction or legitimize change. Sponsors consider the potential changes facing an organization and assess the dangers and opportunities these transitions reflect. They decide which changes will happen, communicate the new priorities to the organization, and provide the proper reinforcement to assure success. Sponsors are responsible for creating an environment that enables these changes to be made on time and within budget.

Agents

An agent is the individual or group who is responsible for actually making the change. Agent success depends on the ability to diagnose potential problems, develop a plan to deal with these issues, and execute the change effectively. The participation of change agents who possess these skills is a crucial factor in the success of any change project.

Targets

The individual or group who must actually change is the target. The term *target* is used because these people are the focus of the change effort and play a crucial role in the short- and long-term success of a project. To increase the likelihood of success, they must be educated to understand the changes they are expected to accommodate, and they must be involved appropriately in the implementation process.

Advocates

An advocate is the individual or group who wants to achieve a change but lacks the power to sanction it. Recommendations to save money or boost productivity can die an early death if those who generate the ideas do not have the skills to gain support from the appropriate sponsors who can approve their ideas.

At different times and in the face of different challenges, you may play the role of sponsor, agent, target, and/or advocate. Many change projects require you to wear more than one hat. It is not unusual for people to say, "I'm an agent for my boss, but the sponsor to my people." The issue is not whether you are a sponsor or whether you are an agent, but in which type of situation you will be a sponsor and under what circumstances you will be an agent.

RELATIONSHIPS

The configuration of role relationships in an organization can take one of three basic forms: linear, triangular, or square. According to how they are managed, each of these structures can contribute to success or lead to dysfunctional behavior.

Linear relationships are represented by the usual management chain of command. The target reports to the agent, and the agent reports to the sponsor. The sponsor delegates responsibility to the agent, who in turn deals directly with the target to assure that the change occurs.

This is not necessarily a successful path to change, but it is easy to understand because it reflects the typical organizational hierarchy: Senior management tells its middle managers to get the employees who work for them to comply with a directive.

Triangular relationships are more complex and, in most situations, largely ineffectual. In the triangular configuration, the

LINEAR STRUCTURE

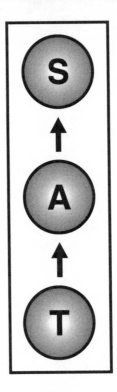

© ODR

Figure 10

agent and the target both work for a common sponsor, but the target does not report to the agent.

A classic triangle is found when the sponsors are senior executives, targets are line managers, and agents work in a support function (such as human resources or information systems). Triangles are not limited to support-function relationships; they are simply good examples of the dynamics involved.

In ODR's research, we have found that as much as 80 percent of the time organizations are not reaping the rewards they should from their triangular relationships. This poor track record

TRIANGULAR STRUCTURE

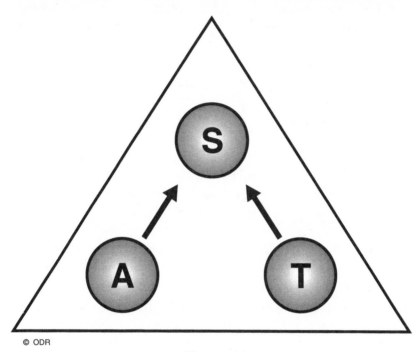

© ODR

Figure 11

stems from sponsors' attempting to delegate to their agents the power to authorize the change. That works fine when sponsors assign to an agent the responsibility of actually rolling up their sleeves and putting the change into effect. However, sponsors cannot pass on sanctioning power to people who do not hold that status with the targets.

Having agents tell targets who don't report to them what to do almost always fails. Such attempts to influence may work for minor changes, but rarely in major transitions. The inappropriate attempts by support staff to pressure line managers into complying with their wishes is at the heart of much of the line-versus-staff conflict so prevalent in today's organizations.

The true culprit in such situations is usually not the support staff, but the sponsors. Sponsors turn to their human-resources director and say, "Go tell the line that they must use the new hiring procedure—that's what I pay you for." Or they say to the head of information services, "Force them to use the new system if you have to—that's your job." In effect, the mandate is to "Tell people who don't report to you what they must do." Of course, when this message meets a brick wall it is the agent who takes the heat for not doing his or her job.

Triangular configurations, however, are not the true source of the problem. Triangles are a natural formation in any organization. The problem lies in too few people understanding the dynamics that govern triangular relationships. You cannot manage such relationships if you do not understand and respect the mechanisms that guide their operation.

I spend a great deal of my time advising sponsors and agents on how to succeed in triangular situations. To sponsors I offer this guidance: Always endorse the change project with the targets yourself *before* you have the agents actually implement the change. Once employees realize that the boss is supporting a particular change, they are much more likely to cooperate.

To agents I strongly suggest that you never take on a project that calls for you to give orders to people who do not report directly to you. In such situations, you may be able to help *facilitate* change, but only after the targets' boss has informed them that she supports it.

In the square relationship structure, agents report to one sponsor and targets to another.

These relationships are also usually dysfunctional in most organizations. The problems occur when Sponsor One directs his agent to bypass Sponsor Two and go directly to the target to gain compliance for a change. Targets rarely respond to major change directives unless these directives come from their sponsor, who controls the consequences applicable to them.

In such situations, Sponsor One and the agent are actually advocates because they have no power to sanction the change

SQUARE STRUCTURE

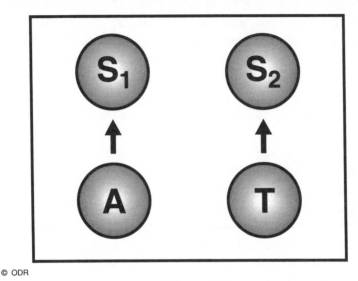

© ODR

Figure 12

with the targets. We have found that unsuccessful advocates try
to directly influence the targets, usually failing because the targets' sponsor does not support the change. For a company's
vice-president of budget and finance to have one of his financial
officers go to the firm's marketing manager to insist on new
cost-cutting procedures is not only ineffective but counterproductive. The finance department's best strategy is for the vice-
president of budget and finance to have his financial officer try
to convince the vice-president of sales and marketing that the
measures are worthy and have her introduce the changes to her
people.

Successful advocates spend their time with the sponsors of
the targets engaging in remedy selling and pain management.
They help the sponsor realize the importance of the desired
change.

EMPERORS WITH NO CLOTHES

All four roles are essential to success, but those in leadership positions are especially significant. Major change will not occur unless the appropriate sponsors demonstrate the sufficient commitment. But do not confuse sponsorship of change with advocacy for change. The fact that a person wants change to happen does not mean that he or she holds sanctioning power with the target population. Anyone can be an advocate: All it takes is what you consider a good idea and the ability to communicate it. Sponsorship takes far more than ideas and rhetoric; it requires the ability and willingness to apply the meaningful rewards and pressure that produce the desired results.

On one of my trips to Russia, I witnessed firsthand the difference between advocates with and without sponsor support. In 1989, I was in Moscow during the first elected People's Congress since the introduction of glasnost and perestroika. The city was buzzing with talk of how newly elected representatives were openly confronting the Communist leadership (including Mr. Gorbachev himself) and living to tell about it. Not only was the majority of the Soviet leadership allowing dissent, it was publicly encouraging this type of debate, saying that it was good for the country.

In contrast, each evening we saw the news coverage of the student struggle for democracy and free speech in Tiananmen Square. In that setting, open dissent was an idea with plenty of passionate advocates but without the sanction of government leaders.

Both China and the former Soviet Union had millions of advocates for major change, but each country achieved radically different results with those advocates. In both countries, the advocates demanded a loosening of strict Communist ideology, an end to authoritarian control, and increased economic freedom. The changes proceeded so rapidly in what was then the U.S.S.R. that the union itself now no longer exists. The advocacy movement in China was stamped out in one day in

Tiananmen Square. The difference between success and failure in both these cases was sponsorship.

Soviet change advocates secured sponsor endorsement from the appropriate levels of power, first from existing leadership (Gorbachev) for radical reform within the existing union and then from new leadership (Yeltsin), to form a new paradigm made up of a commonwealth of completely separate countries. The sponsors, in turn, enlisted change agents, and reform was under way. In China, the advocates succeeded in gaining head-lines but failed to gain sponsorship. The fate of the reform-minded Chinese students clearly showed that the sponsors were the ones with the keys to the tanks.

Successful advocacy has nothing to do with being right. The corrupt and malevolent forces of the world will always dominate the moral and benign as long as they have an endorsement (or legitimization) from those in power.

When sponsors don't fully understand a project's implica-tions or are unwilling or unable to take the necessary action, advocates must either convince the sponsors of the importance of the change, be in a position to replace them with people who will provide the needed support (e.g., a coup or recall vote), or pre-pare for the change to fail. These options reflect the critical role of sponsorship—if it is weak, advocates must educate sponsors, replace them, or fail.

Without the appropriate sponsor's attention, energy, action, and other resources, a major change will remain in the advocacy state or falter after it is announced. If a sponsor believes the change is a business imperative, he or she will probably be highly committed. If the sponsor understands how the change will af-fect the organization, including both its short- and long-term consequences, and can empathize with the targets' experience, he or she will likely sustain this commitment.

A committed sponsor recognizes the demand that a change project makes on organizational resources, including knowledge, time, and money. The resolute sponsor will also publicly com-mit these resources while privately meeting with key individuals or groups to convey his or her resolve to see the change succeed. Such a sponsor will develop reward structures for those who support the implementation and enforce consequences for those who undermine it.

A sponsor shows he or she means business by establishing procedures for tracking the progress and problems of a change project. A strong sponsor is aware that personal, political, or organizational costs always accompany major change, and he or she is willing to pay the price. Finally, a committed sponsor sacrifices other attractive opportunities if they pose a threat to the original goal. The committed sponsor understands that follow-up is a crucial final step for any successful change project.

A good sponsor must have:

- *Power*: the organizational power to legitimize the change with targets.
- *Pain*: a level of discomfort with the status quo that makes change attractive.
- *Vision*: a clear definition of what change must occur.
- *Resources*: a thorough understanding of the organizational resources (time, money, people) necessary for successful implementation and the ability and willingness to commit them.
- *The Long View*: an in-depth understanding of the effect the change will have on the organization.
- *Sensitivity*: the capacity to fully appreciate and empathize with the personal issues major change raises.
- *Scope*: the capacity to understand thoroughly the size of the group to be affected by the change.
- *A Public Role*: the ability and willingness to demonstrate the public support necessary to convey strong organizational commitment to the change.
- *A Private Role*: the ability and willingness to meet privately with key individuals or groups to convey strong personal support for the change.

- *Consequence Management Techniques*: preparation to reward promptly those who facilitate acceptance of the change or to express displeasure with those who inhibit it.
- *Monitoring Plans*: the determination to ensure that monitoring procedures are established that will track both the transition's progress and problems.
- *A Willingness to Sacrifice*: the commitment to pursue the transition, knowing that a price will most often accompany the change.
- *Persistence*: the capacity to demonstrate consistent support for the change and reject any short-term action that is inconsistent with long-term change goals.

Obviously, the demands of being a successful sponsor mean that no one can sponsor more than a few major change projects at a time. Yet losers often engage in far too many change initiatives, draining their time and energy to the point of being unable to adequately perform their sponsor duties.

WHEN THE GOING GETS TOUGH . . .

You can engage change in two different ways: You can initiate it, and you can persist with it. It doesn't take much commitment to initiate change. Losers initiate change every day by sending a memo, giving a speech, or issuing a directive. The real challenge is to maintain the course of change, and the key difference between winners and losers is their resolve to do so. Unless you are acutely aware of the steps to building commitment, you can initiate major change, but it will rarely be carried out.

A prerequisite for committing to change is the recognition that the cost of the status quo is significantly higher than the cost of change. Suppose a man is offered ten dollars to walk ten feet along a two-by-four plank that is two feet off the ground. He would probably say, "No problem." In this case, his commitment to perform the task is easy to attain.

What if the height of the board were raised to twenty feet? Now, ten dollars may be too little incentive for him to risk a broken limb. If the ante is raised to several hundred dollars, it might then be worth it. But unless he really needs the money, he's probably not going to be committed enough to undertake the venture.

What if the height were three hundred feet, across an alley between two buildings? Most people wouldn't try that for even a million dollars. But place a young child on the ledge of the far building, and nearly every parent would be committed to crossing the dangerous height on a narrow board.

In this instance, the price of staying put and possibly watching your baby plummet from the top of the building is much higher than the cost of falling off the board yourself. In fact, most people wouldn't take a million dollars to sit tight and not try to save their child.

It is relatively easy to get your people to acknowledge that a change is to be made and to get started on it. The really tough job is to get them to stick with it when the going gets tough.

In the workplace, initiating sponsors are those with the power to break from the status quo and sanction a significant change. They are generally higher in the hierarchy than those who must perform the duties of the sustaining sponsors. Sustaining sponsors are the people with enough proximity to local targets to maintain their focus and motivation on the change goals.

If an initiating sponsor assumes that a major change will sail through an organization without his or her continual guidance, that change is doomed. The initiating sponsor must be able to enlist the support of sustaining sponsors down in the organization, or the change is certain to fail.

Although it may not seem plausible for a target to ignore a change directive from a senior officer of the company, it is a regular occurrence in most organizations. It usually happens like this: The initiating sponsor of a change is a corporate CEO who makes a videotape announcing the firm's new focus on quality.

The video is shown company-wide. Afterward, the local supervisor says, "Don't worry, it's just a bunch of hot air from the old man." The change is then poised on the edge of an abyss.

Any time there is a gap between strategic rhetoric and local consequences, targets will always be more responsive to the consequences. When the rhetoric the targets hear from senior management is not consistent with the positive and negative consequences that they see coming from their supervisors, a corporate "black hole" forms.

BLACK HOLES

For years, I was frustrated because I didn't know how to adequately describe the problems that occur when change rhetoric does not match what is communicated through consequences. Then in 1985 I began reading about an emerging interest in the scientific community in a phenomenon called black holes. As I became more familiar with the characteristics of black holes, I realized they could serve as an excellent analogy for what happens within organizations in transition.

The expression *black hole* is borrowed from the field of astrophysics, in which it applies to those areas in space that have a gravitational pull so strong that everything—including light—is pulled in. There are spots in the corporate universe that exert the same effect; it is common for management rhetoric to go into bureaucratic structures and then vanish without a trace.

Like the black hole in space that captures everything that travels in its vicinity, various levels of management withhold or distort information so that it doesn't get to the rest of the organization. Without proper information dissemination, change will fail.

The risks to successful implementation inevitably escalate when people's roles in the change process are confused or improperly filled. This is especially true for the sponsor role; successful change must have sponsor support and follow-through.

Of all the factors to consider when estimating the cost of failure—including unsolved problems, missed opportunities, wasted resources, declining morale, and jeopardized job security—disregard for management initiatives is the most significant. When management's efforts at change disappear into a black hole, the price can be devastating.

These voids in the sponsorship chain are so expensive because they cause employee confidence in its leadership to dissipate. When management cannot fulfill the promise of its announced intentions, people learn to associate strategic rhetoric with impotent tactics.

Black holes form where there are local managers who do not adequately support an announced change. This occurs because of unintentional confusion, covert sabotage, or a lack of rewards and pressures directly connected to the change itself. Regardless of the reason, when sponsors fail to display the proper commitment to a change, the targets below them will not fully support the transition.

For instance, say a computer firm's national service director issues an edict for the company's field reps to take the extra time to cultivate more long-term customer relationships (rather than pursue the short-term dollar by rushing to see as many clients as possible during the day). If the national service director doesn't make sure that his district managers are following through with clear, sustained messages and tangible incentives, the change in service orientation will never take hold. The sponsor who originally initiated the project, the national service director, cannot personally ensure that the change occurs at the lower levels of the organization because he does not have the sufficient logistical, economic, or political proximity to the targets. Again, whenever local consequences do not match with strategic rhetoric, the consequences always win.

Corporate black holes contribute to a "change du jour" business climate. If you are a sponsor, failure on your part to match rhetoric with reality severely undermines your credibility. It creates an atmosphere in which people ask: "Will we or won't we?"

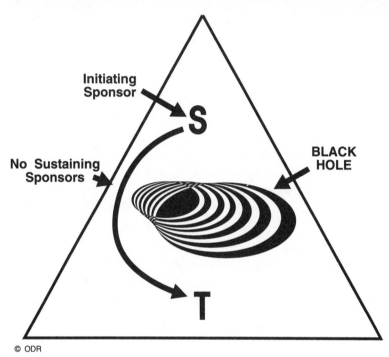

TYPICAL INEFFECTIVE SPONSORSHIP

Initiating Sponsor

S

No Sustaining Sponsors

BLACK HOLE

T

© ODR

Figure 13

After asking that question enough times, attitudes will shift to: "Don't worry; we won't."

This outlook can have debilitating effects on an organization's speed of change, making it too slow to be competitive. The tendency to ignore management directives reduces an organization's response time to major changes, increases the probability of miscommunication and distortion, and minimizes the likelihood of changes being made on time and within budget.

When there is a legacy of poor follow-through, people learn to ignore even bold announcements. The past is a good teacher:

"Another major change? Last year it was leadership by guru, and the year before that it was management by Ouija board."

With ineffective change implementation, an organization cannot execute the strategic decisions necessary to respond to a changing marketplace. Stated objectives are not achieved, and time, money, and human resources are wasted.

When there is poor execution of sound decisions, problems are left unsolved, opportunities are squandered, and morale suffers. But the greatest cost of all is the loss of confidence in the organization's leadership and the perception by others that the leaders are not in control. Such perceptions devastate senior management's capacity to lead in the future and may ultimately jeopardize the organization's long-term viability.

Black holes exist throughout all bureaucracies. From our work around the world, I can report that every organization in every industry in every country is filled with black holes. This pervasive bureaucratic disease, however, seems to be particularly widespread in America.

The lack of credibility of senior-management rhetoric is so problematic for most U.S. companies that it has contributed significantly to the decline of American competitiveness in the world market. American companies still display the old Yankee ingenuity that once made them dominant players, but many are no longer able to execute their creative genius. Craig Weatherup, president and chief executive officer of Pepsi-Cola Company, expressed it this way: "Black holes—everyone in corporate America produces them by the bushel. We found at Pepsi-Cola that we were making a continuous supply of black holes. Then as we understood them better we recognized the extraordinarily high cost of producing this worthless product. Today, we have minimized their occurrence but not without great effort."

Even more sobering is the fact that the leadership-credibility gap caused by black holes is not limited to the organizational arena. At the micro level, too many people no longer believe their teachers, doctors, and clergy. At the macro level, too many people have lost faith in their sports heroes, their congresspeople, and their president.

Whenever there is a discrepancy between your leadership pronouncements and the day-to-day reality of the people you lead, a black hole forms and you lose twice; you not only don't get what you want but you also teach people not to listen to you in the future.

CASCADING SPONSORSHIP

The remedy to the black-hole phenomenon is cascading sponsorship, which begins with the initiating sponsor and ends with the target. Change cannot succeed without a network of sustaining sponsorship that constantly reinforces the importance of a change as it moves through the organization. With cascading sponsorship, initiating sponsors enlist the commitment of other key managers below them to support the change throughout the organization. These managers, in turn, do the same with those below them.

An effective network of cascading sponsors minimizes logistic, economic, or political gaps that exist between layers of the organization, and it also produces the appropriate structure of rewards and punishments that promotes achievement. Reducing the gulf between the rhetoric of change and the incentives and pressures that guide employee behavior dissolves black holes.

Here's a successful cascading sponsorship story. The senior vice-president of marketing and sales for a national telecommunications firm wished to change the way all salespeople in the field reported their projections to the corporate office. As the initiating sponsor, the senior vice-president met with his sales directors to explain the new procedure, treating them first as targets to deal with their resistance and gain commitment. He explained how the new procedure would affect their roles and, ultimately, those of the entire sales force. He also related the change to the corporate vision statement, linked the project with the sales directors' ongoing responsibilities, and provided incentives for following through.

In turn, the sales directors conducted similar meetings with their regional sales managers, first dealing with them as targets to address their concerns, then helping them understand their roles as sustaining sponsors. These regional sales managers had to then convince the sales force to actually change the way they report their projections. Their part was also linked to their ongoing responsibilities and incentives. With this, the change cascaded down through the organization and so the outcome was supported and durable.

Whether at the initiating or sustaining level, sponsors of change must demonstrate strong commitment for transition to succeed. CEO, midlevel manager, or first-line supervisor—all must display a high level of resolve to actually achieve major change, not merely announce it.

ROLE AXIOMS

Based on the dynamics found in this pattern, I offer the following guidelines:

Sponsors

Don't engage in any more change than you can properly sponsor. If you do, you will lose twice—you not only won't achieve the desired results of your change but you will also teach people to disregard your leadership.

Agents

Don't take bad business. Bad business is when your sponsor is unable or unwilling to properly sanction a change with the targets and/or commit to sustaining the resolve necessary to complete the change. When you're involved with a bad-business project, the issue is not "if" the project fails but "when." At that point, you will invariably be blamed.

Also, don't work harder than your sponsor. You should never mask poor sponsorship by acting as a pseudosponsor when the person or group who should be playing that role falters in their duties. When your sponsor cannot or will not take the proper steps to legitimize the change and reinforce the targets, it should be taken as a sign that the project is no longer of sufficient importance to proceed. Let the sponsor know this so that he or she can either adjust priorities or formally delay or terminate the project.

Targets

Don't participate in major change when you are unclear about what is expected of you, the consequences affecting you, and the sponsor's commitment to the effort.

Advocates

Don't confuse the strength of your desire for change with the probability of success. Major change is not possible until it is properly sponsored.

THE FIVE KEY PRINCIPLES IN THE "ROLES OF CHANGE" PATTERN

When involved in major organizational change, you can enhance resilience if you:

1. Understand and can recognize the key roles in a change project.
2. Are familiar with the effective operation of linear, triangular, and square relationship configurations.

3. Understand the general requirements associated with strong sponsorship.
4. Recognize that a change must be clearly and strongly sanctioned by those in initiating and sustaining sponsorship positions.
5. Perceive that the rhetoric of change is consistent with meaningful consequences.

CHAPTER 8

RESISTANCE TO CHANGE

*T*he fourth support pattern is *resistance to change*. When your spouse contests "another" late night at the office or when your child balks at a new baby-sitter, they are resisting change. When those who lose their jobs because of a merger cry "foul" or when managers complain that the quality-improvement program that they demanded is now too time consuming, they, too, are resisting change. We resist change whenever we sign a petition to fight a rezoning decision in our community or stand in a picket line to protest a new school board policy. Resistance is a natural part of the change process; it is the force that opposes any significant shift in the status quo.

When *we* decide to oppose something it is always based on logical thought and "sound" judgment. Yet when *others* fail to support our initiatives, they are "ignorant of the facts," "not thinking rationally," or just plain "troublemakers" who are against anything new. Why the double standard?

It is sometimes difficult to see ourselves or others objectively when we are in the midst of events or issues we consider especially meaningful. But as an outsider invited into many organizations, I am able to view the change process from a more emotionally detached vantage point. From this perspective, I seldom perceive the people struggling with change to be ignorant, illogical, or malicious. They do, however, appear to be altogether human and extremely uncomfortable with situations that disrupt their expectations.

In Chapter 5, I presented human inertia as a compelling force, one that causes people to cling to certainty and oppose any significant interruption of their status quo. Whenever we believe that the challenges we confront differ significantly from the capabilities we possess, we're threatened. Such disruptions in our expectations produce a loss of the psychological equilibrium we unconsciously prize. The resulting stress produces dysfunctional behavior that drains our assimilation capacity and inhibits our ability to absorb change. The greater the discrepancy between the "anticipated" and the "actual," and the longer it lasts, the more severe our dysfunctional symptoms become.

Resistance to change is a natural reaction to anything causing this kind of disruption and loss of equilibrium. Consequently, resistance accompanies any major change whether it is self-initiated or presented by others, and it occurs without regard to how the event was originally perceived—positively or negatively.

We do not resist the intrusion of something new into our lives as much as we resist the resulting loss of control. In fact, the phrase *resistance to change* can be considered somewhat misleading. People don't resist change as much as its implications—the ambiguity that results when the familiar ceases to be relevant.

FRAMES OF REFERENCE

When you attempt to manage change, you lack the luxury of a single, fixed reality. The change process is composed of shifting images, interpretations, and perspectives. To understand and appreciate how another person reacts to change, you must be able to put yourself inside his or her shoes.

A person's perception of a change situation determines whether resistance occurs. What one person sees as a small wrinkle in the status quo, another may regard as a complete transformation.

Professional football players go to work every Sunday and endure levels of physical pain that would put most other people in the hospital. Players may bruise ribs, twist knees, or sprain ankles and yet run back out for the second half after being wrapped with tape. To them it's not even a big deal; it is merely part of their job. From their frame of reference, not going to work due to physical pain would be dodging responsibility.

Your frame of reference is your perception of reality—the unconscious pair of eyeglasses we all wear to keep a fluctuating world in focus. When we think that our ability and willingness to address a shifting situation is sufficient, we feel we can maintain our sense of equilibrium. We feel little need to resist these kinds of changes, because we see them as minor. But when our capabilities are not sufficient to address the problem or opportunity, we start to dig our heels in.

READY, WILLING, AND ABLE

People can only change when they have the capacity to do so. *Ability* means having the necessary skills and knowing how to use them. *Willingness* is the motivation to apply those skills to a particular situation. If you lack either ability or willingness, it is unlikely that you will successfully adapt to a change.

For example, an employee in a computer-chip manufacturing facility was perfectly willing to integrate new quality-control measures into his work but unable to do so effectively, because he lacked the technical background necessary to identify and measure errors. His more experienced partner was able to locate the problems but unwilling to invest the extra time necessary, because she saw no incentive for doing so.

Deficiencies in ability result from inadequate skills and should be addressed by training in the form of formal instruction or informal mentoring. A lack of willingness stems from a shortage of motivation and should be addressed through consequence management (the combination of rewards and punishments).

It is important to remember that to change, a person must both be willing *and* able to do so. These qualities represent two links of a chain and, as the saying goes, a chain is only as strong as its weakest link.

OVERT VERSUS COVERT RESISTANCE

Although resistance during a major change is inevitable, its expression can vary greatly. In some cases, resistance is conveyed overtly. For example, you can resist organizational change through memos, department meetings, one-on-one exchanges, and other public means. Because it is out in the open, overt resistance is more constructive than its underground counterpart; open resistance can at least be heard and addressed, if not resolved.

In other instances, resistance is expressed covertly. When resistance is hidden, it can go unnoticed until it destroys a change project. Behind-the-scenes resistance is usually the result of low trust and inadequate participation. If employees sense that they are not allowed to discuss their true feelings or if they are not involved in implementation decisions, they are likely to feel disenfranchised from the change effort. Many times, these feelings take the form of clandestine unrest—from indirect complaining to outright sabotage.

Where there is major change, there is resistance; but you can minimize negative effects by encouraging resistance to be expressed openly instead of secretly.

Losers fail to realize that *all* major change produces disruption, and *all* disruption produces resistance. Whether the change is viewed as better or worse does not matter. Whether it is a new computer system originally seen as a welcome advance in technology or as the result of emerging competition's invading a company's previously secure territory, people will resist the adjustments required by major change.

Winners increase their resilience by understanding and respecting the natural patterns of resistance. They know resistance is inevitable, and rather than fight it they encourage it. That may sound odd, but we have found that winners do not just tolerate the open expression of resistance, they actually reward their people for resisting in an open, honest, and constructive manner.

The consulting firm of McKinsey & Co. is a prime example of an organization that has built a strong culture based on rewarding open resistance. During my first exposure to this organization, I gained a new level of appreciation for a principle that I had known and taught to clients for years: Open resistance is healthy. After two days of training a room full of McKinsey consultants how to incorporate the resilience principles into their consulting practice, I was exhausted from the intense and constant critique of every concept and technique that I presented. Their response to my material was always professional and polite, but they accepted nothing that I had to say without taking me to task. I am accustomed to challenging and skeptical audiences, but this group was unrelenting in its demand for the supporting evidence behind my findings and examples of application experience.

The two days were intellectually stimulating for me, and their constant questioning forced me to reexamine some of our assertions that had long gone unchallenged. By the time we were nearing the end of the second day, I knew that I had gained a great deal from the sessions. But I was disappointed that the class appeared to have found little value in our change methodology. I had hoped for a more positive response, because the group represented what McKinsey is noted for: They were exceptionally bright, insightful, and had many years of experience helping clients manage change. It would have been nice to have such a group verify that our research supported their own consulting experience.

Instead, it seemed—through the queries and dissection of each element of my presentation—that they had found no use for what I had to offer. In the final hour of the session, the agenda called for feedback and discussion of their overall reactions to the material and how they planned to use it in their consulting practice. I can't say that I was looking forward to the final evaluation.

To my surprise, at this point, the class then shifted in direction and tone, discussing how valuable they found the material and how helpful it would be if they incorporated aspects of our work into what they were already doing to assist clients manage change. To say the least, I was pleased but taken aback. I was then taken aside and given a quick orientation to the McKinsey culture. One of the partners said to me, "Daryl, if you are going to work with us, it is important that you understand the way we operate. The constant challenging that you received the past two days was our way of dealing with you as a peer. Anyone at any level inside McKinsey who stands up to present ideas or new insights is critiqued just the way you were. We're trained from the day that we're hired to question everything. We believe that it's this spirit of inquiry that allows us to help each other push the limits of our knowledge and skills. It is not intended to intimidate but to stretch our frames of reference and make us better consultants."

He then said something that revealed the depth to which their culture reinforces open resistance. "We believe that challenging dialogue is not something to be tolerated; it is something we demand. Dissent is not merely allowed; it is an *obligation* that we owe each other and the company." Resilient people and organizations avoid wasting the energy and potential learning opportunities that occur when resistance is expressed covertly.

Some winners go so far in this approach as to conduct training programs for their targets on "How to Resist Change." These organizations believe that it is inevitable that targets will resist when faced with major change; so the companies choose to instruct their people on how to resist in a manner to which management can relate. This way, resistance can be seen as a valuable aspect of the change process rather than as something to be feared and avoided. Instead of the boxing mentality used by losers—"I'll hit you if you resist me"—winners employ judo mentality—"We can't succeed at this game unless you move toward me."

THE NEGATIVE RESPONSE TO CHANGE

It does not matter whether a change is originally seen as positive or negative; when people's expectations are significantly disrupted, the end result is resistance. But the way people manifest this resistance differs according to how they view the change. Major transitions that are applauded at the beginning follow a pattern distinct from those that are disliked at first.

The most insightful work on the dynamics of negatively perceived change was originated by Dr. Elisabeth Kübler-Ross in her 1969 book, *On Death and Dying*. A psychiatrist by training, Kübler-Ross interviewed several hundred terminally ill patients and their families, eventually developing a means for understanding the process that people undergo as they come to terms with impending death. According to her model, people evolve through a series of stages as they confront their own mortality or that of a loved one.

I had the good fortune of being exposed to Dr. Kübler-Ross and her concepts early in my clinical psychology training. In 1972, when I began to shift my focus from clinical psychology to organizational change, I was surprised to find that her model was just as applicable to the corporate world as it was to a clinical environment.

The emotional highs and lows in her model were less intense in organizational situations, but the sequence of the stages was just as relevant for executives who had to lay off valued, long-term employees as it had been for families of the terminally ill. I realized then that Dr. Kübler-Ross had not simply developed a model for understanding the adjustment to death, but she had also provided a way of understanding any negative change that we face but cannot control.

In more recent years, her work has gained renown among organizational-change practitioners as a way to understand and manage negatively perceived change. Because of the frequency with which this model has been cited or discussed in change-management literature, it is only necessary to highlight the key elements here.

Expanding on Kübler-Ross's five-stage model, I identified eight distinctive stages through which people pass whenever they feel trapped in a change they don't want and can't control. These stages are: stability, immobilization, denial, anger, bargaining, depression, testing, and acceptance.

This model is presented below as Figure 14. The horizontal axis represents the length of time that the person has been aware of the change, and the vertical axis reflects the level of emotional activity that is displayed, ranging from passive to active.

Phase I—Stability

This phase precedes the announcement of the change. It represents the present state, or status quo.

Phase II—Immobilization

The initial reaction to a negatively perceived change is shock. Reactions in this phase may vary from temporary confusion to complete disorientation. Here, the impact of change is so alien to the person's frame of reference that he or she is often unable to relate to what is happening.

Phase III—Denial

This phase is characterized by an inability to assimilate new information into the current frame of reference. At this stage,

NEGATIVE RESPONSE TO CHANGE

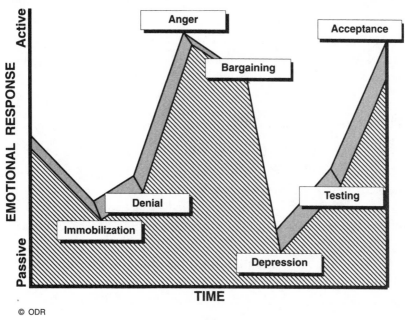

© ODR

Figure 14

change-related information is often rejected or ignored. Common reactions are: "It won't happen to me" or "If I ignore it, it will go away."

Phase IV—Anger

This phase is characterized by frustration and hurt, often manifested through irrational, indiscriminate lashing out. These emotions are typically directed at those in close proximity, who also are usually the ones most willing to be supportive, such as friends and family. So it is not uncommon for those closest to the target to be blamed, criticized, and treated with hostility.

Phase V—Bargaining

Here, people begin negotiating to avoid the negative impact of change. Bargaining takes many forms (e.g., requests for deadline extensions, reassignments). This point in the process signals that an individual can no longer avoid a confrontation with reality. All earlier phases involve different forms of denial. This phase marks the beginning of acceptance.

Phase VI—Depression

Depression is a normal response to major, negatively perceived change. The full extent of clinical depression, helplessness, and hopelessness is not usually found in organized settings, but resignation to failure, feeling victimized, a lack of emotional and physical energy, and disengagement from one's work are likely symptoms here.

   Although it is an unpleasant experience, depression can represent a positive step in the acceptance process. At this point, the full weight of the negative change is finally acknowledged. Given the perceived severity of the consequences, the fact that someone would respond in this manner should not come as a surprise. It may be an uncomfortable period, but it is quite normal for these feelings to surface.

Phase VII—Testing

Regaining a sense of control helps people free themselves from feelings of victimization and depression. They do this by acknowledging the new limitations while also exploring ways to redefine goals; this makes it possible to succeed within a new framework.

Phase VIII—Acceptance

Targets now respond to the change realistically. But acceptance of the change is not synonymous with liking it. It just means that the target is now more grounded and productive within a new context.

Working with targets as they pass through the negative-response model is an expensive process because providing the appropriate support at each phase consumes time and energy. Nevertheless, the price of a valued employee's not being able to complete the sequence can be even more costly. There is no guarantee that people will move successfully through each of the phases on their own. When someone gets stuck at one or more of the phases, dysfunctional behavior typically escalates and can eat up an inordinate amount of assimilation points.

THE POSITIVE RESPONSE TO CHANGE

My first memory of witnessing people resisting a positive change was early in my counseling career when I served on the staff of a rehabilitation center for abusers of drugs and alcohol. I was amazed to learn of the high rate of divorce that took place soon after one partner in a marriage entered the program and began the recovery process. Because I didn't then understand the dynamics of resistance, I could not see why the wife of an alcoholic would put up with her husband's destructive behavior for years only to file for divorce as he began to regain control of his life.

I eventually learned that because the husband was succeeding with sobriety—what the wife had been dreaming of for years—she now had to adjust to his reemergence into the family structure. She had long been making economic decisions and providing sole parental guidance to the children. But once he was fully functioning again, he wanted to participate in these activities. Along with finally getting what she wanted came a power struggle neither of them was prepared to handle. From her standpoint, although his improved behavior was welcome, she was not willing to surrender her hard-won autonomy. The marital roles and family hierarchy became subject to unexpected redefinition. The subsequent power struggle resulted in an abundant source of pessimism for both husband and wife.

Years later when I was working with organizations, this same sort of situation reappeared. I noticed that people who originally perceive a major change to have positive implications follow a separate path of resistance than those who see it as negative from the outset.

At first, it was hard to believe my observations. Organizations that were ineffective at implementing change seemed to be doing what was logical. They would prepare for resistance when they knew that a particular group of targets was going to be upset by a soon-to-be announced project. On the other hand, I noticed winners bracing for resistance regardless of whether or not targets might like the change.

After observing this phenomenon in numerous situations, I was finally able to describe the phases people go through when they originally embrace a change perceived to be positive, only to resist later.* The five phases of positive resistance to change are:

1. Uninformed optimism;
2. Informed pessimism;
3. Hopeful realism;
4. Informed optimism; and
5. Completion.

In Figure 15, the horizontal axis represents time once again, but the vertical axis reflects the degree of discomfort or pessimism felt toward the change.

---

* My thanks to consultant and poet Don Kelly for his insight and willingness in 1974 to introduce me to this way of viewing the negative implications of positive change.

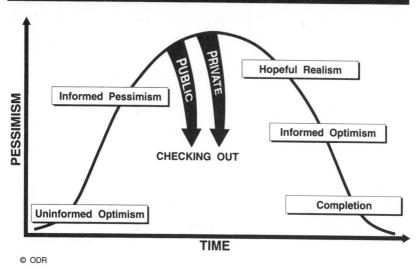

Figure 15

Marriage is a classic example of a major positive change that people think will be great in the beginning but then have trouble adjusting to. When people first get married, they haven't spent much "married" time together, so they are on the left-hand side of the time continuum. And they are on the low end of the pessimism scale because they usually feel extremely positive about each other and their decision to be together. Instead of the "honeymoon," we call this phase "uninformed optimism." It is a naïve enthusiasm based on insufficient data.

Getting married fits into the same change dynamic as a long-awaited merger/acquisition, introducing "breakthrough" technology to an organization, or the hiring of a consultant who management thinks will have the cure for all its problems. Major change decisions are always based on information that will later prove to be inadequate. As these changes unfold, we learn that a great deal of what we were promised does not come to pass, and much for which we were not prepared begins to take place.

Over time, a couple discovers some of the real prices for their change decision. He learns how often she wants to eat out; she learns how often he wants to play golf. They begin to realize that while their overall decision may have been a good one, there are significant costs accompanying this decision that they did not expect.

There is no way to avoid this second phase of the process; it comes from the inevitable learning that takes place once we engage a positive change. "Informed pessimism" always follows uninformed optimism. It is impossible for it not to happen. I know that it's dangerous for a researcher to say that something "always" happens, but the evidence from our observations is overwhelming. We do not have a single documented case in which a major change that was originally perceived as positive didn't generate at least some second thoughts and doubt—the basis for informed pessimism.

The informed-pessimism stage is a source of concern because every person has a certain tolerance for pessimism. If a person's pessimism exceeds that tolerance level, however, "checking out" occurs. Informed pessimism is a doubting of the change decision; checking out is a withdrawal from the change decision.

Checking out manifests itself either publicly or privately. You can check out publicly by displaying overt checking-out behavior. In the marriage situation, coming home to one's spouse and delivering a blunt statement such as "I filed for divorce yesterday" is an example of public checking out. Or you can check out privately by going underground with your detachment. Many couples go through the mechanics of their marriage, but the genuine exchange of respect, admiration, and passion is gone. A person who privately checks out undergoes the same tensions as the person who checks out publicly.

Both types of checking out jeopardize the success of a project, but the public form is clearly less destructive than the private. At least with public checking out, there is an acknowledgment of the problems. With private checking out, emotions are dangerously hidden.

Although informed pessimism is inevitable, checking out is not. Whether or not a person checks out depends on each individual's tolerance for pessimism. Some people are ready for a divorce within two weeks of getting married, others can beat each other up for thirty years and never seriously consider separating.

If checking out never takes place or if it occurs openly and the problems are brought to the surface and resolved, the concerns of informed pessimism begin to taper off. But the pessimism does not suddenly disappear. Instead, the pessimism lessens and you move into "hopeful realism." This isn't a return to the "Everything is wonderful" days of uninformed optimism; it simply means that you begin to see light at the end of the tunnel.

In the hopeful-realism stage, you still have a great number of issues to handle. But you begin to feel as if "Maybe we can pull this thing off." As more and more concerns are resolved, you become increasingly confident and move into the "informed-optimism" stage. This stage reflects a strong confidence that has been earned through trial by fire.

As you know, a marriage, like any major change, does not have just one of these cycles. A couple goes through the positive-response-to-change cycle when they are first getting used to being married and again when they embark on another seemingly good idea, such as having their first baby. Then one of them decides to go back to school, there is the long-awaited promotion and the family's relocation to another city, the best friend that comes for a long visit, and the decision to build that dream house.

Life presents a series of apparent "home runs." Home runs happen when you expect to receive a tremendous benefit from an action that is inexpensive and poses little risk. Most of us devote a great deal of our lives trying to hit (find) these home runs, and there are plenty of people out there willing to pitch (sell) them to us.

The trouble is that, outside of baseball, home runs seldom occur. Anything of real value has a price tag. We are not obligated to buy what we say we want, but if we do, the invoice will soon follow. Naïveté—thinking that perfection sought can be inexpensively obtained—often leaves us unprepared for the inevitable disenchantment and doubt that develops after we achieve our goals and the bill comes due.

There is a wonderful scene in the film *Out of Africa* when the character played by Meryl Streep realizes that after a long struggle she and Robert Redford's character will finally come together. Although elated, she also recognizes that the much-longed-for relationship will breed problems of its own. At that moment, she says, "When the gods are angry, they answer your prayers." The lesson here is: Be careful of what you pray for, because you might get it. And then what would you do? Remember, there are no panaceas for managing change.

The saying "You always get what you pay for" applies to positive as well as negative change. Those wonderful, positive things that happen in your life are invariably expensive. You either pay for getting what you want, or you pay for not getting what you want. But you *will* pay.

One of the key lessons from this positive response to change model is that most of us long for these mythical home runs only to discover that they are more costly than we anticipated. If the cost is too high, we withdraw from the decision; if the doubt and subsequent pessimism do not exceed our tolerance level, we are usually able to resolve our concerns and move ahead.

SUCCESS THROUGH SOBER SELLING

Both the negative and positive response to change models reinforce the idea that we seek control, and that we fear and avoid the ambiguity of disruption. The negative-change model confirms what everyone, even losers, know: People do not like what they cannot control. The positive-change model is often the source of more insight, because it uncovers dynamics typically hidden from us. We do not expect problems to accompany the things that we have always wanted.

Winners know that surprises are inevitable anytime there's a major change—even if it's positive. Losers, unaware of this, tend to consume assimilation resources by being surprised that they were surprised. Such people are particularly vulnerable to those who are looking for an easy mark to sell their false home runs to. These panacea merchants play on people's fantasies of reaping big returns with small, no-risk investments.

Major changes are often described like this: "I have a great new software package that will triple productivity. It only takes a half hour to read the manual, and it costs just $29.95." With that kind of rosy picture, who's going to fight the change? Of course, the reality is that anything that good has more implications to it than meet the eye.

One main reason why so many change projects fail is that people have such unrealistic expectations. Whether out of ignorance or by design, when "sellers" of change find an overly naïve "buyer," checking out is likely to occur at a later point.

One of the most devastating things you can experience is being surprised at life's surprises. When you realize that something *might* happen, you can to some degree prepare yourself, even if unconsciously. It is another thing altogether to have no idea that what just happened to you was even possible.

To manage change well you must use *sober selling* as your approach. In the early stages of a project when enthusiasm is high, you must intentionally tell targets what the true costs of the change will be. You can say something like: "This is a wonderful change, or I wouldn't suggest it to you. But nothing in life that's this good is cheap. To realize the overall benefit, there are going to be some costs involved. Let's prepare for them."

This sober-selling approach not only increases the likelihood that people will get through the informed-pessimism stage, it establishes early on whether or not they have the resolve and/or the resources to move through the entire process. But there is a risk associated with this approach. If you honestly explain to people the real price of change, they may not attempt it. Most people are only interested in major change (even for the better) if it's cheap.

Because I spend much of my time helping people orchestrate change, this next statement may sound odd. I am as proud of the number of times that I have talked clients out of embarking on a major change as I am of the number of times that I have helped clients implement one. I feel this way because I have learned from winners that it is essential to divulge up front the real price for change.

The risk you run with this level of honesty is that, if presented with the full cost of change, some people will not pursue certain initiatives. But these people would not have sustained their efforts anyway; they would have checked out as soon as the true cost for implementation surfaced and their own tolerance for pessimism was exceeded.

How many people do you know who would not have married had you been able to show them the true price of matrimony before they walked down the aisle? I can tell you how many just by looking at the divorce rate.

A divorce simply means that someone decided that the cost of being married was higher than the cost of not being married. If someone makes that decision while he or she is dating, it is called good judgment. If it is made after they are married, it's called divorce. It is the same decision; it's just a matter of timing.

If you help people realize early the price of change, you can accomplish one of two things: First, you help them decide whether or not they actually want to pursue the change. Second, if they do want to pursue it, you have helped them build the resolve necessary for getting through the inevitable pessimism. You have enabled them to anticipate to some degree what it is that they are going to experience.

Anticipating informed pessimism does not mean that you

can circumvent it. You will still be surprised when things happen that you did not fully expect. But since you know such things are at least in the realm of possibility, you are not as surprised that you were surprised.

Say that you have a major argument with your spouse that you had anticipated having before the two of you got married, but you had decided at that time that sharing your life with that person would be worth the chance of having that argument. You are surprised the dispute is happening now, but you are not completely floored that such an argument has occurred. You are not saying to yourself, "This is crazy. We're not supposed to argue—we're married." You are saying, "That's right; this is part of the price for being together that I knew we were going to pay."

In the business environment, it may be a situation where you have tried for a long time to convince senior management of the benefits of viewing customer service as an investment rather than as an expense. Because of stiff new competition, they are now agreeing with you and have approved your plan to refocus the entire organization toward a service mentality. Soon after telling you how wonderful your idea is, however, the boss begins to falter in his time commitments to the project and gives a few people mixed signals about his resolve for the objective.

As these events begin to unfold, you don't storm off the project in amazement and surprise. Instead, you remind yourself: "It wasn't *if* but *when* the pressure of other projects was going to wear down some of the boss's initial enthusiasm. I've got to keep him on board as the competition for his attention becomes greater."

Losers are at a disadvantage because they are devastated when life throws them curves. Winners understand that by definition major change entails surprises. When overwhelmed by a surprising surprise, victims of change waste many of their assimilation resources, reducing their ability to absorb change efficiently and effectively. By "expecting" surprises during change, winners are able to minimize the number of assimilation points needed to deal with the disruption. Through understanding the movement from uninformed optimism to informed pessimism, resilient managers are able to reduce the risks of positive change because they are better prepared to soberly evaluate and prepare for its costs. They do not waste their resources by being overly naïve and caught off guard when what appears to be a positive change produces unexpectedly negative implications.

When the chief information officer (CIO) of a major manufacturing operation in Brazil heard me describe the benefits of not being surprised at inevitable surprises, he told me about the time he was promoted into his current position. He said that it had taken him years to persuade his CEO and the other senior officers that the company's information systems should be managed like any other strategic resource.

Finally convincing them of the merits of this approach, he was promoted to the CIO role and reported directly to the CEO. He said that along with the achievements he had worked so hard to accomplish came a set of surprises that nearly cost him his job and his family: A much higher level of demand was made on his time; he learned through working closely with the CEO that his new boss had mood swings that he had never noticed from a distance; he was now on a bonus system tied to the profitability of the company and an industry-wide slump was eroding the increased compensation he had anticipated; and these issues had caused his home life to be tense and unfulfilling.

He said that he eventually worked his way out of or adjusted to most of the stressful issues, but not before a great deal of anguish and turmoil had all but consumed his assimilation capacity. As he finished the story, he confided that the single most draining aspect of all this was not that it happened, but that he was so unprepared for it. Because he was unprepared, he invested an inordinate amount of his assimilation resources denying that those things were taking place or blaming himself or others for their occurrence. Neither of these activities generated the problem-solving behavior necessary to cope with the disruption.

His story reinforces the fact that resistance is inherent to disruptive change; the only variables are how and when it is manifested and what is done with it. Ambiguity is always accompanied by a resistance invoice. You can pay early or late, you can pay for managing it or healing from it—but you will pay.

THE FIVE KEY PRINCIPLES IN THE "RESISTANCE TO CHANGE" PATTERN

When involved in major organizational change, you can enhance resilience if you:

1. Understand the basic mechanisms of human resistance.
2. View resistance as a natural and inevitable reaction to the disruption of expectations.
3. Interpret resistance as a deficiency of either ability or willingness.
4. Encourage and participate in overt expressions of resistance.
5. Understand that resistance to positive change is just as common as resistance to negatively perceived change and that both reactions follow their own respective sequence of events, which can be anticipated and managed.

CHAPTER 9

COMMITTING TO CHANGE

Successful change is rooted in commitment. Unless key participants in a transition are committed to both attaining the goals of the change and paying the price those goals entail, the project will ultimately fail. In fact, most change failures trace back to this lack of commitment, with obvious symptoms like sponsors terminating projects or more subtle signs such as target apathy serving as leading indicators. The fifth support pattern is *commitment to change*.

You can make all the right moves and still strike out with change. A new procedure can be implemented on the surface but still fall far short of the sponsor's expectations. In other words, the operation was a success, but the patient died.

As the work environment becomes more complex, organizational change demands more from sponsors, agents, and targets than mere adjustment and compliance. Regardless of their roles in the change process, winners recognize the level of commitment required for the changes that will make their businesses succeed. Losers typically underestimate the commitment these

changes demand or attempt them knowing full well that sufficient commitment is unattainable.

Your commitment to a specific outcome is evident when
you:

- Invest resources (time, energy, money, etc.) to insure
  the desired outcome.
- Consistently pursue the goal, even when under stress and
  with the passage of time.
- Reject ideas or action plans that promise short-term benefits but are inconsistent with the overall strategy for
  ultimate goal achievement.
- Stand fast in the face of adversity, remaining determined
  and focused in the quest for the desired goal.
- Apply creativity, ingenuity, and resourcefulness to resolving problems or issues that would otherwise block
  the achievement of the goal.

Given that committed people will devote the time, money,
endurance, persistence, loyalty, and ingenuity necessary, it is
easy to see why commitment is critical for successful change. It
is the glue that provides the vital bond between people and
change goals. It is the source of energy that propels resilient
people and organizations through the transition process at the
fastest, most effective pace possible—the optimum speed of
change.

THE STAGES OF CHANGE COMMITMENT

Even though building target commitment is essential for major
change, few sponsors and agents seem to understand how to
develop it or how easily it can be eroded. After many years of
observing people either strongly commit to certain change initiatives or falter during implementation, we have been able to
identify three specific stages in the commitment process: *preparation, acceptance,* and *commitment.*

STAGES OF CHANGE COMMITMENT

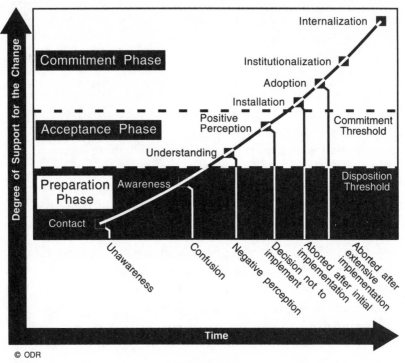

Figure 16

The vertical axis of the commitment model (Figure 16) displays the degrees of support for a change, and the horizontal axis shows the length of time someone has been exposed to a change. Each of the three phases—preparation, acceptance, and commitment—represents a critical juncture in the commitment process. The model shows how the degree of support for a change can progress or regress as time goes on. You can track the process of building commitment according to the points at which a change can be threatened (indicated by downward lines) or advanced to the next upward stage.

PREPARATION
Contact

The preparation phase of the commitment model has two stages: contact and awareness. Your first encounter with imminent change varies according to your role in the change process. For example, if the change is a new marketing strategy, the sponsor (the CEO) could have his initial exposure to the necessity of change while reading a weak financial statement. The agent (the marketing director) might have first contact with the impending change through a senior staff person who has discussed the problem with the CEO. The targets (the sales force) will have their first contact with the change in the form of a new sales approach presented by the marketing director at a staff meeting.

Contact efforts—whether they come in the form of meetings, speeches, or memos—do not always produce awareness. There are two possible outcomes of the contact stage: *unawareness* and *awareness*. Unawareness reduces the chances of adequate preparation for commitment. Awareness, of course, advances the preparation process.

Awareness

You pass into the awareness stage of the commitment process once you realize that modifications affecting your operations are in the works. Nevertheless, as with the contact stage, awareness does not necessarily mean that someone has a complete understanding of the change's full impact. In many cases, targets know that a change is coming but are at the same time confused as to the specific effect the change may have on them. They may be unclear about the scope, nature, depth, or even the basic rationale for the change.

The two possible outcomes for the awareness stage are *confusion* and *understanding*. Confusion reduces the likelihood of adequate preparation, whereas understanding advances the process to the second phase—acceptance.

ACCEPTANCE

Understanding

Understanding the nature and intent of the change is the first portion of acceptance. People who are aware of and comprehend the change are now able to judge it. Nevertheless, the outcome of this judgment will be based on each person's perception of reality, which varies according to his or her own intellectual and emotional viewpoints and values.

Once people begin to think and act in certain ways toward the change project, they have crossed the "disposition threshold." A positive perception of the change signals progress into the acceptance phase. Negative perceptions indicate resistance to the change. Nothing is ever black or white, so change of any significance produces both positive and negative reactions. A change may be perceived as negative from one aspect but still be accepted because of a stronger, more positive implication. For example, a target may have a negative view of a new company policy that requires relocation every four years. But she goes along with this change to achieve job security. The target eventually accepts the change as primarily positive, even though some negative perceptions may remain.

The development of a predominantly negative perception at this stage is the first opportunity in the commitment process for true target resistance. Failure to pass through the earlier stages may produce unawareness or confusion, but not resistance. Targets will engage in resistance actions (either covertly or overtly) only after they have formed a negative perception of the change. Sponsors and agents often respond to unawareness or confusion as if they were symptoms of target resistance. These are signs of resistance only when they are feigned and thus part of a resister's strategy. Actual resistance develops only if the person has enough understanding to form a perception and judgment.

The possible outcomes for the understanding stage are *neg-*

COMMITTING TO CHANGE 151

ative perception and *positive perception.* A negative perception decreases support and provides an environment that may foster true resistance. Positive perception increases support and the likelihood of change acceptance.

Positive Perception

Once you perceive a change as positive, you must decide whether or not you are going to support it. It is one thing to view a new procedure as positive but quite another to decide on committing the necessary time, energy, and other resources to make it work. As a sponsor, you might view a prospective change as useful and still prefer not to implement it. In such a case, your positive perception would take a back seat to the feeling that the potential return is too low compared with the high cost of implementation.

Unlike sponsors, targets and agents don't function as decision makers regarding change, but they do decide how much of their personal support they will lend to a particular change. Most organizations have learned the hard way that reluctant agents and targets can stop a plan that they do not fully support right in its tracks. Management-employee alienation, reduced productivity, decreased quality, absenteeism, grievances, and even overt sabotage are all possible symptoms of agent or target resistance to change.

Once you perceive a change as positive, you are ready to move on to the commitment phase. But how you manifest this commitment will differ according to your role as sponsor, agent, or target. Sponsors use their organizational power to legitimize the change and ensure that it takes place. Agents actively carry out the sponsor's decision. Targets support the project willingly and are involved in the steps necessary to fully carry it out. The two possible outcomes of the positive perception stage are either *a decision not to support implementation or a formal decision to initiate the change.*

COMMITMENT
Installation

Once you decide to embrace the change in some fashion, you have entered the fifth stage of the commitment process: installation. The project is now operational, and a second milestone has been reached—the "commitment threshold." The installation stage is not only a pilot period in which the change is tested for the first time; it is where the first opportunity for true, committed action arises. And this action requires consistency of purpose, an investment of resources, and the subordination of short-term objectives to long-range goals.

Given that this is a trial period for the change, problems are inevitable and some degree of pessimism is unavoidable. But a work environment that encourages the open discussion of such concerns tends to solve problems and build commitment to action. As the difficulties are resolved, a more realistic level of conviction toward the change develops. This conviction is what allows commitment to advance to the adoption level. There are two possible outcomes for the installation stage: Either *the change is aborted* after initial implementation, or *it is adopted* for longer-term testing.

Adoption

Though the dynamics of installation and adoption are similar, there are important differences between the two stages. Whereas installation is a preliminary test focusing on start-up issues, adoption examines the extended implication of the change. It focuses on in-depth, long-term concerns. A considerable degree of commitment is necessary for organizations to reach the adoption stage. But a change project in this stage is still being evaluated—cancellation is an option. Typical reasons why change projects are aborted after extensive testing are:

- Logistic, economic, or political problems were found that could surface only after a significant testing period.

- The need that sparked the initial commitment no longer exists.
- The overall strategic goals of the organization have shifted and now do not include the change outcomes.
- People in key sponsorship or agent positions have left the organization or are not as active in the project as they once were.

There are two possible outcomes for the adoption stage. The change can be *terminated* after extensive use. Or the change can be *institutionalized* as standard operating procedure.

Institutionalization

Installation and adoption are short- and long-term test periods, respectively, in which turning back is still an option. Moving beyond the testing point means the question is not whether the change will be made, but how. Once the project has been institutionalized, employees no longer view the change as tentative. They expect to use it as a matter of routine. It is now the norm, not, as in the past, a deviation.

Once institutionalization occurs, the organizational structure alters to accommodate the change. Also, rewards and punishments are put in place to maintain the change. What was once a project requiring substantial sponsor reinforcement becomes an integral facet of the operational system. While institutionalization is indeed a positive development for many change projects, it can often contribute to problems. A theme that has become woven into the fiber of an organization can be extremely difficult to eliminate. If a change has been institutionalized, people may adhere to the procedures merely to comply with their bosses' wishes.

For example, many change projects become institutionalized when targets are given the option to comply or face severe consequences. Despite their own private beliefs about the change, the targets are motivated by reward or punishment to conform.

When targets already have a negative perception of the effort, this strategy usually has little positive impact on their attitudes toward the change. In these situations, targets simply mimic acceptable behavior. They learn to say and do the "right" things. They are like the little boy whose parents demanded that he eat his green beans: "You can make me eat 'em, but you can't make me like 'em."

Nevertheless, the success of change does not always depend on the target's personal belief. Some projects only require that the new task be physically accomplished, with or without emotional support. But as the pace of change escalates and produces more disarray in the workplace, many organizations are reevaluating their beliefs that targets need not understand or emotionally support major organizational changes. Management has begun to realize that such an attitude typically results in half-hearted and inefficient implementation efforts that fail to produce a full return on investment. Institutionalization is powerful, but it only alters target behavior; it doesn't win their hearts. The outcome reflects bodies, not souls.

Internalization

When employees are highly committed to a change because it reflects their personal interests, goals, or values, the ultimate level of commitment forms—internalization. This is commitment that comes from the heart. For a change to achieve maximum support, employees must be driven by an internal motivation that reflects their own beliefs and desires as well as those of the organization. The company may legislate the institutionalization of a change, but the targets control their own internalization.

When targets internalize a change, they "own" the change. They contribute deep-seated advocacy and take personal responsibility for the project's success. No organizational mandate could ever generate this sort of individual investment in a change. Enthusiasm, high-energy involvement, and persistence are the stuff of internalized commitment. This behavior tends to be infectious. Usually, targets who have internalized a change are so devoted to a project that they engage others in the effort. This enthusiasm makes them hardly distinguishable from sponsors in terms of their emotional investment in the change.

GUIDELINES FOR COMMITMENT

The lack of full commitment to change is one of the prime reasons winners are so rare. Building commitment to change is not easy, and the process is something for which many people are not prepared.

Resilient organizations do not take commitment to change for granted. Nor can you. They approach the development of strong commitment to new initiatives as an understandable and manageable process. Here are six guidelines crucial to building the commitment necessary for successful organizational change:

1. *People respond to change at different intellectual and emotional rates.* As we adjust to organizational change, we typically enter a pattern of:

- observing that a change has occurred or is possible;
- developing our opinion toward the change;
- making a decision to support or resist the change; and
- taking action on that decision.

Our heads and our hearts move at different rates. The capacity that we have to intellectually observe, form an opinion, decide, and act is greater than our capacity to move through the same sequence emotionally. Therefore, as we participate in organizational change we often make an intellectual commitment that far exceeds our emotional one. Such split-level commitment produces confusion among targets, and sends mixed signals to sponsors and agents.

A classic example of this problem occurs when a sponsor

moves too quickly to the institutionalization stage. The sponsor pushes through a new procedure only to find that, once in place, the change produces more human-relations problems than anticipated. Even though he accepts the responsibility intellectually, the sponsor is not emotionally prepared to confront his angry employees. Few people are ready to deal with resisters when they actually see the red faces and clenched jaws of irate colleagues.

As a manager of organizational change, you must learn to deal with both the intellectual and emotional cycles of commitment, taking into consideration the differences between the two as you develop your implementation plans.

You must also distinguish between deteriorating commitment and the mixed messages that people produce when their heads have accepted the change, but their hearts are still struggling.

2. *Commitment is expensive; don't order it if you can't pay for it.* Gaining organizational commitment is both complex and costly. Most sponsors want full support for the changes that they hope to make, but they have little understanding of the effort and expense involved in acquiring it.

Successfully developing strong commitment is largely a matter of facing up to its real cost. Once sponsors confront the heavy investment of time, money, and energy required to generate commitment in others, they often balk. They want the benefits associated with high target support, but they are not willing to pay the price to earn them.

The days are gone when managers could say, "I don't need to tell my employees anything, listen to their input, or give them special rewards. They work for me. If they know what's good for them, they'll do exactly as I say . . . or else!" Today's more sophisticated workers and complex corporate environments make it easy for people to kneel at your feet in obedience, then bury your project when you turn around. Whenever possible, avoid covert resistance by paying the price for target commitment.

As indicated below, you will either pay for commitment or you will pay for resistance—but you *will* pay.

	Commitment Payments	Resistance Payments
Price of Resistance	Paid early	Paid later
Initial Investment	High	Low
Maintenance Cost	Low	High
Initial Implementation Speed	Slow	Fast
Ultimate Speed of Assimilating Change	Fast	Slow
Target Investment	Bodies and souls	Bodies but not souls
Target Motivation	Project success	Compliance
Commitment Level Achieved	Internalized	Institutionalized

3. *Don't assume commitment will be generated without a plan of action.* Managers often devote considerable resources to making the right decision about what should be changed, and then fail to build the commitment necessary to execute that decision. For burning-platform issues, change implementation is too risky to leave commitment to chance. A well-thought-out strategy will increase the probability that targets will commit to such an imperative change.

Strategies for building commitment should not be limited to targets only, however. Sponsors must develop plans to ensure that their agents are fully supportive. Agents in turn often need to increase the level of sponsor support for programs that these same sponsors originally initiated.

Of course, not all change projects require the same level of commitment. Some entail only trying out the new format or procedure. This usually calls for a commitment to installation only. Other projects must go through an extensive testing period. This requires a greater degree of commitment—that found in adoption.

For many change projects, the intent of the effort will be lost unless the change becomes formally sanctioned and, if necessary, legislated to assure compliance or institutionalization. Finally, if the long-range goals of a change demand high levels of support from employees, the maximum level of commitment—internalization—is necessary. This takes place when there is an alignment of individual and organizational value for the change.

Losers typically lack a plan for building commitment, or if they have one it is only for when the installation is announced. If the organization's change demands internalized support, yet management is only able to develop commitment through force, the project will falter. It would be like cutting short a golf swing at the point of contact. Without adequate follow-through, a change project that appears on course could wind up mired in a sand trap.

4. *Keep in mind that building commitment is a developmental process.* A firm resolve toward change goals can only occur if you view the commitment process from a developmental perspective. The stages leading to commitment are sequential in nature. For example, awareness is the result of successful contact, and understanding must occur before you can generate positive perception.

Obviously, sponsors can attempt to skip some stages by simply announcing that a change has already been institutionalized. With this approach, the announcement is made, behavior is dictated, and compliance is assumed. Most organizations still handle major change in this fashion.

Forcing compliance may assure the technical implementation of a change, but often sponsors neglect to calculate the long-range cost of recurring resistance. Many times, the way people are approached—rather than the change itself—is what causes resistance. A common response from targets is, "We didn't mind the new procedure so much as the way management handled the situation."

If you are operating in a safe, stable industry, you can better afford the risk of bulldozing your changes through. In the 1950s and 1960s, that is how many U.S. business changes were made. In those days, American economic, industrial, and military might ruled the world, making change decisions less complicated. But when U.S. managers assess today's global competition and the implications of sophisticated initiatives, they realize that skipping even a single step in the commitment process can doom a critical change project. Major change demands major commitment. And if one company doesn't build it, its competitors will.

5. *Either build commitment or prepare for the consequences.* A change project's importance to the organization and the degree of disruption it causes should determine the level of commitment required for success. The greater its significance and attendant disruption, the greater the amount of commitment required.

Inevitably, there will be situations in which high levels of commitment are preferred, but its cost is too high. When full commitment is not feasible, your only choice is to prepare for resistance.

Too often, sponsors and agents decide not to invest in building target commitment, and then they are surprised and unprepared for the inevitable resistance. You cannot stand on both sides of the fence at the same time. Sponsors and agents must either do what is necessary to build target support or develop a response to the ensuing resistance.

6. *Slow down to increase the speed.* Sometimes it appears that the swiftest way to implement change is to force it. But this approach only appears quick because most people do not calculate the cost of long-term, covert resistance. There is an interesting paradox that we have observed among resilient people and organizations: By slowing down, it is possible to have the time for opening communication, involving employees, fostering empowerment, and developing synergistic working relationships, thereby generating genuine commitment to the desired change. Winners report that these activities take time at the beginning of an effort, but they say that the process inevitably moves faster to

full implementation than was otherwise possible. Commitment is time consuming and expensive to attain. But once its infrastructure develops, the speed of assimilation can accelerate.

THE FOUR KEY PRINCIPLES IN THE "COMMITMENT TO CHANGE" PATTERN

When involved in major organizational change, you can enhance resilience if you:

1. Realize the sequence of steps involved in committing to something new.
2. Are provided with the time and appropriate involvement to become emotionally as well as intellectually committed to a change.
3. Are sponsored by people who invest the time, resources, and effort to assure specific plans are developed that will increase the likelihood people will commit to change.
4. Understand that commitment to a major change is always expensive, and that you either pay for achieving it or pay for not having it.

CHAPTER 10

CULTURE AND CHANGE

*T*he sixth basic pattern supporting resilience, *culture and change,* concerns the influence corporate culture has on the final outcome of any change effort. Culture is the frame of reference that helps distinguish one group of people from another. Culture establishes a unique set of formal and informal ground rules for how we think, how we behave, and what we assume to be true. While individual members of a culture are distinct in many ways, their collective viewpoint serves as a common bond.

The number of companies and institutions that must drastically alter their cultures to survive has risen dramatically in the last few years. In the early 1970s, there were only a few organizations that were earnestly attempting to shift some aspect of their cultures. In the past ten years, as corporate culture has become a hot topic in the business press, the number of organizations intrigued with attempting some form of culture change has steadily increased. In fact, the idea of changing one's corporate culture is now so in vogue that it would be embarrassing for an upwardly mobile manager to show up at a cocktail party without being able to engage in conversations about the latest "culture project."

There's nothing surprising about the fact that many organizations have been seduced into thinking that changing their culture is the latest quick fix. There will always be fads that people temporarily embrace and then cast aside. What I find interesting is the number of executives who are earnestly depending on radical cultural transformation to save their jobs or even their companies' future. They realize that cultural change for their companies is not a quick fix, fad, or luxury; they must either accomplish it or their company will cease to be a key player.

In the past, true cultural change was rare because a typical organization faced only one or two issues a year, if any, that seemed to indicate a cultural change was necessary. Today, it is not unusual to work with an executive group that faces expanding global competition, increasing customer demands, fewer financial resources, outmoded technology, inadequate organizational structures, a disenchanted work force, and a commitment to quality and customer service that is academic rather than oriented toward actual results. Any one of these problems would justify a perfunctory examination of the culture, but the combination of crises makes the need for culture change truly urgent.

CULTURAL WINNERS AND LOSERS

Over the years, I have witnessed a number of change projects slam head-on into an organization's culture, never to rebound. Corporate culture is a tough opponent to go up against, and winners and losers approach it in totally different ways.

Losers who manage change too slowly to successfully compete say things like, "Culture doesn't really exist. It's a fabrication consultants invented to generate fees," or "Culture is real, all right, but it has nothing to do with the bottom line. It's that soft, mushy stuff the human-resource people play with," or "It's real and it's important, but it's an act of God. You can't really do anything about it. If you're lucky, you get a good one. If not, you're stuck."

I hear the opposite from winners at the executive level. They say things like, "Culture is an essential element of our equation for running the business," or, "Of course it can be managed. It's not easy, but orchestrating the culture is a key element to my role as a senior manager." Winners operate on the basis that clusters of people and even whole societies have their own ways of understanding the world in which they live. Designing a culture sensitive to that world view while assimilating the changes a company faces is one of the techniques winners use to manage changes at a competitive speed.

A major function of any culture is its self-preservation. When the culture is a social one, its perpetuation protects the language, ideas, customs, and manners of dress and behavior unique to that society. Likewise, corporations strive to preserve their cultural boundaries.

CULTURE AS CORPORATE IDENTITY

Corporate culture is an organizational self-concept roughly analogous to individual personality. Like its human counterpart, an organization's self-image develops over a long period of time (although the basic elements coalesce during the organization's formative years). A company's culture is actually an aggregate of subcultures that have developed in response to unique challenges faced by different groups within the organization. This is why corporate culture is inherently so multifaceted and complex.

The concept of organizational culture has spawned many experts, who offer an array of definitions and approaches to the phenomenon. Since my interest in the subject centers on the relationship of culture to change, I will offer a definition that has proven helpful from that perspective.

The following characteristics are crucial for understanding the relationship between culture and change.

1. *Culture is composed of three components.* The prevailing *beliefs, behaviors,* and *assumptions* of an organization serve as a guide to what are considered appropriate or inappropriate actions to engage in for individuals and groups.

2. *Culture is shared.* It provides cohesiveness among people throughout an organization.

3. *Culture is developed over time.* An organization's existing culture is the product of beliefs, behaviors, and assumptions that have in the past contributed to success.

The above principles form the basis for the following definition of culture that ODR uses in its research: **Organizational culture reflects the interrelationship of shared beliefs, behaviors, and assumptions that are acquired over time by members of an organization.**

Beliefs

Beliefs are the set of integrated values and expectations that provide a framework for shaping what people hold to be true or false, relevant or irrelevant, good or bad about their environment. Whether in oral or written form, belief statements can entail both intended and unintended messages regarding what people plan or think they should do.

During a consulting engagement with one of the large drugstore chains in the United States, I observed the testing of an interesting cultural belief. In reviewing the company's corporate mission statement with senior management, I came upon the following line: "We intend to pursue any and all means to reach the profit objectives that can be accomplished within the retail structure now in place." I sensed that they had not fully discussed the implications of the statement, so I suggested that they open massage parlors in the back of each store. They would then meet their criterion of a 20 percent return on their investment, and the parlors could be introduced as a special section in the stores already in place so that no new outlets would be required. Management immediately decided that its statement needed to be more specific so that it could reflect certain values and beliefs that the company holds dear.

Behaviors

Behaviors are observable actions that constitute the way people actually operate on a daily basis. Whereas beliefs reflect intentions that are often difficult to discern, behaviors can be verified in a more objective manner. Where people park, who they do and don't talk to, what they wear to the office, how decisions are made, and how conflict is managed are the kinds of behaviors associated with an organization's culture.

Assumptions

Assumptions are the unconscious rationale we use for continuing to apply certain beliefs or specific behaviors. When people develop belief and behavior patterns that are successful, they rely on those patterns when similar circumstances arise. If such situations occur repeatedly, these patterns eventually become routine and are applied with less conscious thought. When this occurs, we refer to the patterns as "unconscious assumptions."

One of my clients in the United Kingdom told me this story about assumptions. He said that when the British Army first faced the Gatling gun (the ancestor of the modern machine gun) in battle they were stunned by the enormous number of casualties that it inflicted. In the nineteenth century, the British troops still marched onto the battlefield in long lines to face the enemy. Their bright uniforms and antiquated tactics cost them five hundred men in a matter of minutes against the rapid-fire Gatling gun. The last battlefield communiqué from the field commander reveals the way preconceived notions can block our creative problem solving. The communiqué requested, "How are we going to get another five hundred men?" For the field commander, there was only one way to march into battle. Replacements were his only concern; alternative maneuvers were not considered.

An organization's collective beliefs, behaviors, and assumptions affect daily business operations on two levels: the overt level, representing observable, intentional, and direct influences on operations (e.g., goals, policy-and-procedure manuals, and corporate philosophy statements), and the covert level, characterized by obscure, unintentional, and indirect influences on operations (e.g., informal ground rules, unofficial guidelines, or "the way things are around here"). These latter influences are difficult to change because they sometimes lie below the surface of our awareness, and/or we may be reluctant to discuss them openly.

On the overt level, an organization operates along the lines of its beliefs and observable behaviors. At the covert level, the organization is influenced by people's collective assumptions. Though the combination of these elements can be blatant or subtle, culture is a true part of organizational life that can be conveyed by a number of practices, including:

- oral and written communications, such as presentations and memoranda;
- organizational structure as reflected by line and staff relationships;
- the way power and status are defined both formally and informally;
- what is measured and controlled, such as time and quality;
- formal policies and procedures found in employee manuals and official communication;

- reward systems, such as compensation plans and supervisory techniques;
- stories, legends, myths, rituals, and symbols, such as company heroes, award banquets, and corporate logos; and
- the design and use of physical facilities, including how space is allocated and furnished.

Whether the influence is unstated or directive in nature, a corporation's cultural beliefs, behaviors, and assumptions serve as a powerful means for defining, justifying, and reinforcing business operations. This self-fulfilling cycle is depicted in Figure 17.

Culture provides ways for employees to understand important decisions. Based on this understanding, expectations develop that limit possible responses. Because of these responses, employees make certain decisions and behave in accordance with those expectations, confirming and reinforcing the culture's original patterns. This process reinforces a strong corporate identity but can also restrict the introduction of new beliefs, behaviors, and assumptions that may contribute to success in a changing environment.

To effectively align your company's culture with a decision to change often requires developing beliefs, behaviors, and assumptions that are consistent with the new resolutions. For instance, if a company requires a new set of skills from its employees that is dramatically different from those rewarded in the past, some cultural shift may be in order. Say that a company's move to a customer-driven culture requires more decentralized decision making. The firm's employees would have to take on more responsibility for on-the-spot problem solving and creative customer service. A company that hadtraditionally reinforced rigid bureaucracy and central control would have to work hard to break out of its old habits in order to become increasingly market responsive. This company would have to develop new beliefs about the value of creativity and customer

SELF-FULFILLING CYCLE

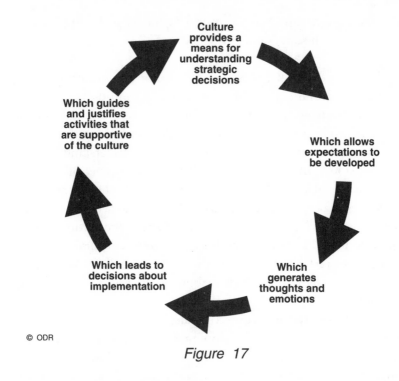

Culture provides a means for understanding strategic decisions

Which guides and justifies activities that are supportive of the culture

Which allows expectations to be developed

Which leads to decisions about implementation

Which generates thoughts and emotions

© ODR

Figure 17

service over procedure and control; management and employees alike would have to learn new behaviors that are more in tune with the market; and they would have to form new assumptions more appropriate to working in the newly directed organization. The eventual outcome should be the alignment of the culture with the change strategy.

During periods of major change, cultural boundaries are seriously strained. While this has always been true, the increasing volume, momentum, and complexity of change in combination with the shifting demographics of today's work force are intensifying the challenge of maintaining cultural cohesion.

CULTIVATING A CULTURE

Few cultures develop from a carefully constructed plan. Most unfold over the years without conscious design, a result of the many policies and decisions that have accumulated over time. Evolutionary development of culture is the unplanned emergence of beliefs, behaviors, and assumptions. These cultures emerge from a history of isolated decisions made under particular circumstances, generating a default corporate culture.

For example, years ago the sales management in a high-tech firm believed that personal contact with clients was essential. They found that by following up visits with handwritten letters their sales increased. Now the organization believes that such personal letters are less important to their sales strategy. A higher volume of contacts seems more valuable in today's market. So the organization purchased a system to automate follow-up letters. But the system was installed without a thorough explanation or any incentive to learn how to use it. To management's surprise, the salespeople continued to write letters by hand, despite the fact that word processing would increase the volume of contacts and sales.

In this case, the old culture was inconsistent with the new sales strategy. Moreover, since the old culture was not consciously developed, management was at a loss to explain why the salespeople continued writing their letters by hand. It never crossed their minds that altering the firm's cultural messages would lead to the successful change.

There are those more resilient organizations that intentionally create a culture that best serves their needs. Architectural development of corporate culture is the conscious design and maintenance of a set of specific beliefs, behaviors, and assumptions. Here, culture is carefully planned and implemented to achieve success as defined by management.

For instance, suppose that a different firm—one with an architecturally oriented management team—decided that they, too, wished to boost the volume of their sales contacts. Before implementing the technological change to increase volume, it would be necessary to alter the appropriate cultural variables. Beliefs about what constitutes successful sales would be modified to incorporate word-processing systems. This would be reinforced through explanation and consequence management. A higher volume of contacts and increased sales would result as the old culture was altered to be consistent with the new sales strategy.

The following comparisons depict further distinctions between these two approaches to cultural development.

Evolutionary	Architectural
Reactive	Proactive
Reinforces beliefs and behaviors developed in the past.	Reinforces beliefs and behaviors needed to support present and future strategy.
Allows for multiple, inconsistent beliefs and behaviors.	Establishes multiple, but consistent, beliefs and behaviors throughout the organization.
Subcultures form that represent potentially contradictory beliefs, behaviors, and assumptions, resulting in destructive conflict.	Subcultures form that represent different beliefs, behaviors, and assumptions, but they operate synergistically to support one another.
Unconscious assumptions are the strongest influence on the success or failure of change.	Conscious beliefs and behaviors become the most important determinants of success or failure.
Culture is difficult to manage because it is composed primarily of assumptions, which are covert and difficult to change.	Culture is more manageable because it is composed primarily of beliefs and behaviors, which are overt and are more easily measured and changed.

EVOLUTIONARY CULTURAL DEVELOPMENT

When development is evolutionary, culture is unplanned, emerging in reaction to sporadic short-term needs rather than according to a long-term view. New beliefs and behaviors develop to meet those challenges and, subsequently, successful ones are reinforced. Eventually, the beliefs and behaviors are taken for granted and evolve into assumptions. Once this occurs, these now familiar beliefs and behaviors are no longer questioned, becoming business as usual.

As time passes, people repeatedly draw on these successful solutions, many of which were developed during the founding period or during crises in the organization's history. This process creates a complex configuration of beliefs, behaviors, and assumptions that establish the culture. While some of these beliefs, behaviors, and assumptions continue to be appropriate, many outlive their shelf life. Some of these may begin to have a negative impact on the business. Such unguided development fosters multiple, inconsistent cultural messages that encourage the growth of contradictory subcultures (which may result in destructive conflict).

Evolutionary cultures rarely drive new strategic initiatives successfully. Current changes within the banking industry are a case in point. Several years ago, many commercial banks made the strategic decision to enter investment banking. Most have found the transition difficult. The cultures of these banks had developed without conscious design during a relatively predictable market environment, and they were typically centralized and bureaucratic. Rigid policies and procedures developed to minimize the risks associated with transactions made repeatedly over the years.

Such rigid cultures are inconsistent with the need to respond quickly in a fast-moving market. Many transactions today are unique; hence, rules governing one transaction are often inappropriate for the next. Although a commercial bank's decision to enter investment banking may have been correct, unless it alters its culture to be consistent with the requirements of investment banking, the transition may fail.

Evolutionary response to new initiatives is a hit-or-miss proposition. Instead of a planned alignment between culture and change, this implementation strategy often degenerates to the "spray-and-pray" approach (i.e., take your best shot then stand back and hope for the best). In these situations, strategic decisions are not likely to be well implemented, and their results are poor or mixed at best.

ARCHITECTURAL CULTURAL DEVELOPMENT

In contrast to the high risk of the evolutionary approach, some corporate cultures develop architecturally. This process consists of intentional planning that consciously orchestrates the culture, increasing the likelihood that it supports the necessary changes.

Although divergent subcultures also form in this type of cultural development, the architectural approach fosters supportive interactions between them—not destructive conflict. Also, an architectural culture is more manageable due to the public nature of its beliefs and behaviors.

The primary steps involved in the architectural process are:

- Senior management defines the specific characteristics of the desired culture.
- Management then conducts a "culture audit" to determine the gaps between the existing culture and the one desired.
- Management identifies detailed action plans to close the gaps.
- Management engages in a structured implementation of those plans.

THE NECESSITY OF MANAGING CULTURE

Although the term *corporate culture* has become an accepted part of today's management vocabulary, few executives use culture to their full strategic advantage.

If an organization's cultural environment is not managed well, people will feel that changes are coming at a greater volume, momentum, and complexity than they can adequately assimilate. These feelings hinder the process of absorbing change for many organizations. **A key element to enhancing resilience and minimizing the chance of dysfunctional behavior is to actively manage your organization's culture.**

Lack of cultural management has been catastrophic for some companies. The combined effect of a quantum leap in business changes and the inability of management to understand and orchestrate the cultural infrastructure to support these changes has generated problems of crisis proportions in many organizations.

A large telecommunications company's decision to enter the volatile computer industry provides a particularly good illustration. The organizational changes required by this decision included much more aggressive marketing and entrepreneurial risk taking than in the past. But born under the umbrella of government regulation, the company had a bureaucratic culture that could not respond with the speed necessary in fast-paced high-tech markets. Often months passed between the time a deal was structured and corporate headquarters approved it.

Although most of the strategic decisions appeared appropriate, implementation failed because the established culture was ineffective in a deregulated market. It's not that strategic initiatives were ignored; they simply did not make sense to people when viewed from the old cultural perspectives.

Another example: In recent years, hospital and other health-care organizations have learned that they must become more customer focused. Consequently, they have become more aggressive in their marketing and sales efforts and are taking a close look at the way they service their clients. For such changes to succeed, the culture must be modified to provide the necessary human support system.

You can't change a culture without strong resolve from top management and a wide-angle view of the situation. Developing a plan to implement a new definition of customer relations, for example, must include clear statements of vision (why the organization exists), mission (what it is going to accomplish), and strategy (how it is going to work toward its objectives). Assessing the degree of consistency between the existing culture and the kind of culture needed to implement the change is critical to the success of any new organizational focus. If the existing culture is inconsistent with the beliefs, behaviors, and assumptions necessary for success, that culture must be altered or the effort will fail.

Here's a final example of the impact culture has on change. Though most attempts at mergers and acquisitions concentrate on the integration of material assets such as capital, facilities, markets, technology, and products, blending cultural elements is often more crucial to success.

A number of the CEOs we have interviewed state that a lack of cultural integration is a major reason why their attempts to complete mergers or acquisitions fail to achieve the intended goals. Although many have mastered the tangible facets of such transitions, most fail to consider the intangible, human factors until it is too late.

For example, Company X is a conservative, old-line manufacturing company that has just acquired a competitor, Company Y. Company Y is renowned for both its cutting-edge research and development and its humanistic operating style. The latter company has a "work hard–play hard" ethic, with liberal provisions for flex-time, on-site day care, and profit sharing. But Company X, in merging Company Y's operations with its own, has concentrated on the technical facilities and eliminated many of the humanistic considerations of flexibility and creative autonomy that made Company Y thrive. As a result, many talented workers have chafed at the new rigid, stifling atmosphere. They resent the fact that "big company" rules and procedures have superseded the fruitful, collegial atmosphere that they worked so hard to cultivate. Productivity has dipped drastically and turnover has risen; the expected value of the merger has not come to be.

Problems in mergers and acquisitions typically stem from such a misalignment of two cultures and are compounded by a lack of skill for cultural management on both sides. When cultures are misaligned and poorly managed, change inevitably fails.

Essentially, there are three basic types of working relationships that will produce a positive cultural environment after a merger or acquisition agreement is reached:

1. *Coexistence*: Here, two separate but mutually supportive cultures work in sync. A new organization is added to the framework of a larger or more powerful business, but it is expected to operate with maximum autonomy and flexibility. The alignment of the cultures is minimal and may be restricted to the corporate level of the business.

2. *Assimilation*: The dominant culture prevails here, either through natural attraction or greater strength. For the acquisition to succeed, one company must alter its culture by aligning with the dominant culture of the other.

3. *Transformation*: While coexistence and assimilation represent options for acquisitions, this third alternative is available only to companies attempting a merger. A true merger results when two or more companies integrate their resources to form a new, more powerful entity that represents a substantial change from either of the previous organizational cultures. This involves identifying strengths from each organization and exploiting them to create a synergistic union.

Any of these three options represents a legitimate strategy during the transition of a merger or acquisition. But it is critical to avoid a fourth common outcome: rejection. This is usually the case when the change effort results in separate and hostile cultures—marked by resistance, territorial contentions, miscommunication, lack of trust, little cooperation, missed opportunities, malicious compliance, and even sabotage. I was brought in to consult in one situation in which these conditions lingered for years after the merger agreements were signed.

Unless managers gain the necessary skills for integrating two or more previously separate cultures into an effective working relationship, merger-and-acquisition efforts will either fail outright, produce performance well below expectation, or succeed much later than anticipated and cost much more than planned.

CULTURE AND CHANGE

Your organization's cultural traits must be consistent with what is necessary for driving new decisions, or those decisions may not be successfully implemented. But the overlap between the existing beliefs, behaviors, and assumptions and those required for your changes to succeed may vary greatly.

If your organization's current culture and the change you want to make in the company have little in common, your chances of successfully achieving that change are slim. The odds of implementing your change grow as the similarity grows between the existing culture and the beliefs, behaviors, and assumptions required by the new initiative.

Whenever a discrepancy exists between the current culture and the objectives of your change, the culture always wins. The effective management of your corporate culture is an essential contributor to the implementation success. It cannot be left to chance.

Because it is durable and resistant to major change, corporate culture requires the investment of a great deal of time and resources before it can be modified. Some people try for years to

HOW CULTURE IMPACTS CHANGE

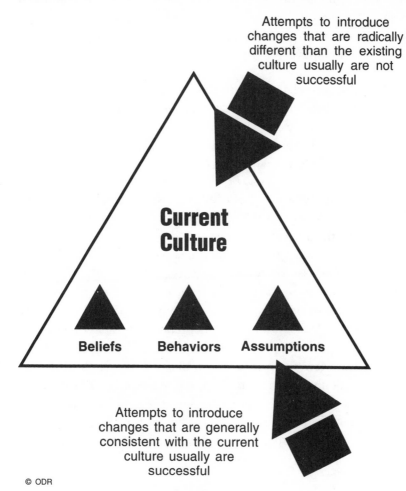

Attempts to introduce changes that are radically different than the existing culture usually are not successful

Current Culture

Beliefs   **Behaviors**   **Assumptions**

Attempts to introduce changes that are generally consistent with the current culture usually are successful

© ODR

Figure 18

cut the dandelions and other weeds from their lawn. These attempts are always in vain. Only by attacking the root of the problem can you eliminate it entirely.

You will encounter minimum resistance when a change initiative is consistent with your current organizational culture. When facing an organizational culture that may hinder a desired change, your options are to:

- modify the change to be more in line with the existing beliefs, behaviors, and assumptions of your culture;
- modify the beliefs, behaviors, and assumptions of the current culture to be more supportive of the change; or
- prepare for the change to fail.

The same dynamics hold for large-scale social change. For example, the former Soviet Union faced three alternatives: It could dramatically scale back the stated objectives of perestroika to protect the status quo; it could transform the country's beliefs, behaviors, and assumptions to be more consistent with a free-market economy; or it could watch the economic revolution fail. With the dissolution of the union, the toppling of Gorbachev, the ascendancy of Yeltsin, and the emergence of the new commonwealth, it's apparent that it was the U.S.S.R.'s culture, its leadership, and even the structure of the country itself that was radically redefined to help foster the new reforms. Resilient organizations view their cultures as key resources crucial to the success of major change. They realize culture is an aspect of business operations that can be guided and orchestrated in the same way other strategic assets are managed.

THE THREE KEY PRINCIPLES IN THE "CULTURE AND CHANGE" PATTERN

You enhance resilience during major organizational change when you:

1. Understand the powerful effect culture has on the outcome of any major change effort.
2. Know that major changes introduced into an organization must be supported by the organization's overall culture and its local subculture.
3. Recognize that when countercultural changes are introduced, you must alter the existing culture to support the new initiative.

Part IV

ONE PLUS ONE IS GREATER THAN TWO

*T*he chapters in Part III described six of the seven support patterns dealing with the nature, process, and roles of change, resistance and commitment to it, and the cultural implications of change. I also identified key principles from each of these support patterns that, if followed, will enhance resilience and advance the speed of assimilating change. The seventh support pattern is the *synergy pattern* and the subject of the next two chapters.* Synergy exerts a powerful influence on the other six patterns, and its importance to the final outcome of any major change effort makes it necessary to discuss it separately.

How people relate to each other during change determines their individual and collective abilities to absorb the implications of what is happening. Synergistic relationships between spon-

---

* My thanks to Dr. Charles Palmgren for first introducing me to this way of viewing how resilient people relate to each other and for the many years of having access to his insights as we both struggled to better understand this phenomenon.

sors, agents, targets, and advocates serve as "the ties that bind" during the challenges of change. The synergistic process is the cornerstone of managing change successfully, laying a foundation for all the other principles of resilience.

Whether the setting is a marriage, a management team, or an entire nation, when two or more people combine their resources to accomplish a change-related task, the nature of their relationship is key to the effort's success or failure. Part IV focuses on the working relationships between those playing the key roles during organizational change. The following two chapters will describe the dynamics of the synergy pattern and identify the critical principles for promoting resilience.

CHAPTER 11

PREREQUISITES TO SYNERGY

*B*efore you attempt to make a change, you must examine the relationships among the project's key sponsors, targets, agents, and advocates. These relationships can be viewed as self-destructive, static, or synergistic.

SELF-DESTRUCTIVE RELATIONSHIPS

In self-destructive relationships, one plus one equals something less than two. When the two parties interact, they consume more resources than they produce and the result of their joint effort is a net loss. Often, people in self-destructive relationships spend most of their time miscommunicating, blaming, being defensive, and complaining about why they can't make headway on the task. Each party drags down the productivity of the other. They consume so much energy in conflict with one another that the combination is worse than if each party had worked alone.

This relationship is considered self-destructive because it

does not generate enough resources (productivity, profit, progress, positive feelings) to sustain itself. These relationships can maintain themselves on a long-term basis only if they are subsidized. This is equally true for a company in which the more profitable divisions subsidize the weaker ones, or a marriage subsidized by extramarital affairs.

Self-destructive relationships consume so much energy trying to recover from miscommunication and self-serving behavior that there is little energy left for the joint creative problem-solving efforts that would lead to increased productivity. For instance, a corporation's weak division has so much infighting that its employees have no time to deal with their customers. It can only survive with aid from the parent organization. Or the married couple experiences so much discontent that one of the partners pursues an extramarital affair to satisfy unmet desires, and the couple only stays in the marriage "for the kids," economics, or other reasons.

A key feature of a self-destructive relationship is that the people involved use the negative situation to justify behavior that would otherwise be unacceptable. If a money-losing division in a large corporation had to stand on its own, it probably would be revamped. Instead, because the other divisions cover for it, the losses continue. In a marriage, the same happens when a dissatisfied partner is unwilling to live with the duplicity of an affair. If that person's morals prohibited having an affair, he or she would probably either resolve the troublesome issues or dissolve the marriage. Justification by subsidy often allows dysfunctional behavior to continue that would normally not be tolerated.

STATIC RELATIONSHIPS

Static relationships involve an even mix of unproductive, back-stabbing behavior and productive, team-oriented behavior. In contrast with self-destructive relationships, people here are about as effective working together as they would be working alone. This is an instance of one plus one equaling two. Sometimes they detract from each other's individual performance, and sometimes each complements the other to achieve somewhat more than he or she would have alone.

We call these static relationships because they barely remain afloat and do so only in calm seas. Although participants in a static relationship are able to generate some productivity, their noses are just above the waterline. Static relationships produce just enough to get by, but not enough to generate the excess resources necessary for significant productivity during change.

The danger in static relationships lies in their apparent safety. Participants can grow complacent, believing they can tread water indefinitely. They may be able to do so as long as they don't have to confront change. Change is inevitable, though, and when it occurs it is a resource-consuming activity—it devours assimilation points. So, when a static relationship encounters change, the weight of its nonproductive stalemate drags the participants below the surface.

Those in a static relationship may be able to stay above the waterline for a while by working harder and harder. But they cannot sustain this extra effort forever. Since ever-increasing change is a fact of life, a static relationship has little chance of long-term survival and no chance of prosperity.

People in static working relationships trying to function in shifting environments experience increasingly larger gaps in their defenses against the disruptive effects of change. Events that used to be manageable now seem confusing and exasperating. The resulting disorientation consumes more and more resources as people attempt to regain their equilibrium. Since no surplus exists, the resources to address change must come from what was to be used for productivity. Thus a destructive cycle continues until the status of a $1 + 1 = 2$ relationship degenerates into the $1 + 1 < 2$, or self-destructive state. Those who lose when facing major change typically relate to one another in one of these two ways, while winners usually engage in 1 + 1 > 2 relationships.

THE SYNERGISTIC BUSINESS RELATIONSHIP

Synergy is the soul of a successful change project. In a synergistic relationship, individuals or groups work together to produce a total effect that is greater than the sum of their separate efforts. In these cases, one plus one is greater than two.

Synergistic relationships are like combining iron, carbon, and nickel to make steel. None of the elements alone could do the job of the alloy, but the blend is much stronger than the sum of its parts. Similarly, in a healthy marriage the husband and wife create a mutual support system so that together they can engage in providing love and support for one another, fostering each other's growth, parenting, generating income, and weathering circumstances that might be too burdensome individually.

Synergistic organizational relationships enjoy the cushion of surplus assimilation resources, which enable people to increase their resilience and successfully deal with major change. During times of relative stability, synergistic relationships produce a cache of assimilation points to weather the next storm of change. Even when unexpected changes are thrust upon them, they may not need to tap their reserves because their continual production of resources is often sufficient—they simply divert some of them toward implementation of the change.

Since synergistic relationships need not fear transitions as a threat to their survival, they are free to seek change rather than cower from it. Synergistic organizations are confident that they can implement change in a manner that maximizes their odds of success. This confidence leads them to pursue necessary change much earlier than those intimidated by its possibility. Instead of waiting for an emergency to respond, these organizations anticipate and choreograph change.

A strong correlation exists between successful change implementation and synergistic teamwork among sponsors, agents, targets, and advocates. Orchestrating major change to best take advantage of available skills and resources provides a significant competitive edge. One of the characteristics of a resilient organization is that it has more assimilation points available than others who fall victim to future shock. Synergistic relationships help produce this competitive advantage because they consume the fewest assimilation points, use their implementation resources wisely, and are able to manage change at a speed appropriate to the surrounding disorder.

How can you create and enhance synergistic teamwork? Read on.

THE SEEDS OF SYNERGY

There are two prerequisites for the development of synergy within a relationship: *willingness* and *ability*. Willingness stems from the sharing of common goals and interdependence. Ability is a combination of empowerment and participative management skills.

Willingness

Although synergistic relationships are powerful and productive, they are neither easy to develop nor inexpensive to maintain. Powerful, effective teamwork comes only with the willingness to invest hard work and perseverance. For example, a common myth about teamwork is that it requires members to always agree and see things the same way. While social harmony makes for a nice appearance and pleasant conversation, it does not necessarily promote creativity. Diversity, with its tendency to generate disagreements, contributes much more to creative thought. Without the natural conflict of different viewpoints, there is no grist for the mill—even though everyone may get along wonderfully. Healthy, productive conflict among people with different perspectives leads to creative synergy.

Some problems and opportunities are so complex that without creative, synergistic approaches they cannot be adequately addressed. But synergy requires teamwork, and many people tend to hold fast to their independence. For some, admitting that they need the help of others to accomplish a goal is tantamount to ego suicide. These people do not deal well with changing environments.

People who like to fly solo can perform well in circumstances not requiring teamwork. For instance, boxing or singles tennis is not a team sport; it requires the ego and self-sustaining capability of someone like Evander Holyfield or Martina Navratilova to succeed. Teamwork, on the other hand, requires shared insights and ideas, open discussion, and respect for the values and input of others.

We have found that the only time people are motivated to pay this price is when the parties believe that they need each other to achieve mutually desired outcomes. Common goals and interdependence form the foundation for synergistic willingness. Because synergy is difficult to attain, people are only willing to move beyond their sense of self-containment when it becomes obvious they will fail at something valuable if they don't function with others as a team.

Although there has never been a time of true racial harmony in the United States before or since, racial tension peaked in many U.S. cities and institutions in the 1960s and 1970s. This strife was particularly evident in the military, where prejudice, intimidation, and violence were common to both blacks and whites. But in Vietnam during a firefight, if a black soldier and white soldier shared a foxhole and one had the weapon and the other had the ammunition—you would not believe how well they worked together. This was because under those conditions, they shared a common goal (survival), and they knew that without genuine cooperation (interdependence) they would not achieve that goal.

When people who have diverse viewpoints acknowledge that they have the same intent and are willing to be interdependent, they display what we refer to as "foxhole mentalities." Foxhole mentalities are not limited to the life-and-death circumstances of combat. Family members, managers and employees, and world leaders can determine that their differences are less important than their need to work together.

An illustration of the foxhole mentality can be found in the cooperation between certain American and Japanese automakers. While competing strenuously for market share in a tough economy and hotly debating such issues as trade protectionism, some American and Japanese companies have realized that it is in their best interests to work together on joint ventures. Sharing design methods, engineering technology, and manufacturing philosophies, automakers such as Chevrolet and Toyota have learned to improve their products and industry relationships by investing in cooperative projects. The common goal of quality improvement and the interdependence brought on by a tight economy have provided the foundation for synergy between would-be competitors.

If some catastrophe or dire market condition befalls an organization putting its survival in jeopardy, few managers have difficulty seeing their interdependence with each other. A foxhole mentality is not limited to negative situations, however. Common goals and interdependence can occur as the result of powerful opportunities, which would not be realized without synergistic teamwork.

Leaders today face the challenge of building genuine teamwork between sponsors and targets, employees and managers. The critical element with which they must deal is the price for failing to operate synergistically. A foxhole forms when the cost of operating as a team is less expensive than functioning separately.

Since the international sanctions against South Africa began to ease in early 1990, ODR has been actively involved with business, government, and special-interest-group leaders as they attempt to manage the incredibly complex set of issues surrounding the paradigmatic shifts necessary for the "new South Africa" to succeed. By any rational analysis, the task is too massive and convoluted to succeed. And yet, not only is the number of people who believe that they must succeed growing, but the number who think there is a unilateral solution is diminishing. I have been consistently impressed with a wide range of business, governmental, and social leaders whose foxhole mentalities are flourishing.

The task of forging a new framework for a multiracial social, economic, and political model in South Africa is formidable. Despite the magnitude of the challenge, each time that I am in the country I meet more and more people who are convinced that the price for not crafting a genuinely synergistic coalition is prohibitively high. Such resolve does not guarantee success, but without such passionate commitment a $1 + 1 > 2$ national equation is impossible. A growing number of South African leaders seem to feel that they are on a burning platform.

Organizational leaders facing major change must reach the same conclusion about the need for synergy. People in lower echelons often feel the hazards of daily operations and changes more quickly than those in higher positions. A CEO will eventually confront a miscalculation, but the people who work for him or her farther down in the organization are in a position to provide advance warning. If the CEO is uninvolved and detached from the lower echelons, he or she will miss this valuable input.

True teamwork in organizations is often a function of economic, logistic, or political foxholes that convince people that they not only have the same goal but that they need each other to accomplish it. A key challenge for today's manager is either to exploit naturally formed foxholes or build new ones that will foster successful teamwork.

The biggest barrier many managers face in digging foxholes is their own fear of losing absolute control over their area of responsibility. To these people, a shared power situation is threatening. Most executives who really share power are the ones who realize that they will not get what they want if they refuse to cooperate. It comes down to a simple choice: Do you want to feed your insecurities, or do you want to succeed in a world that has grown too complex for leaders to deal with alone?

An irony that often destroys the opportunity for synergy is that managers are unable to admit that they are in a foxhole and cannot succeed alone. The work force is hired for the unique skills and perspectives that it brings to the job. Yet once people begin to work, the managers who hired them punish them for offering innovative ideas or disagreeing with the status quo.

When workers feel that they are in a foxhole situation with the boss at their side and that success depends on working together, then synergy can occur. If you give those working for you the sense that they are the ones carrying the ammo, it boosts their feeling of self-worth: "The company needs me, and I need the company; we must work together to survive in today's volatile business environment." But employees must view these managerial overtures for teamwork as authentic. Rhetoric and token participation will not suffice. Managers must be willing to say and *mean,* "I'll listen to you even when you give me information I don't want to hear. Why? Because you're the one with the bullets. I need you."

The biggest barrier employees face in digging foxholes is their reluctance to accept responsibility for asserting their opinions. Many people have felt so impotent in their personal lives and throughout their careers that they are hesitant to engage with management in a truly empowered fashion.

Regardless of the difficulties faced by management and employees in developing these foxholes, sponsors, targets, agents, and advocates must believe they are all striving for the same goals and are genuinely interdependent. This bond motivates people to pay the price for a synergistic relationship.

Ability

Common goals and interdependence make people willing to work together synergistically, but that's not enough. For syn-

ergy to thrive, the individuals involved must also demonstrate
the skills to operate in an empowered manner, and the organization must demonstrate its readiness to appropriately involve
employees in change-related decisions affecting their work. *Empowerment* and *participative management* are the two key abilities
people must possess to operate synergistically with one another.

EMPOWERMENT

Empowered employees are those who provide true *value* to the
organization, influencing the outcome of management's decisions and actions. The antithesis of empowerment is victimization. Victims believe they are faced with a negative situation
offering no alternatives. In actuality, most victims face alternatives they refuse to act on because they view them as too expensive.

Victims resent feeling as if they are being used and tend to
feel depleted by change. Therefore, they demonstrate little interest in contributing beyond what is necessary to protect their
employment during unsettled times. Subsequently, the organization profits little, if any, from its investment in such people.

For foxholes to form, employees must overcome their fear
of victimization and engage management in an empowered fashion as key contributors to a team effort. The basis for this approach is not blind faith, but the knowledge that they hold
management's bullets, which provides a healthy balance of power
in the relationship.

Empowerment Should Not be Confused with Delegation, Courage, or Autonomy

Empowerment Is Different from Delegation
Many organizations mistakenly refer to "empowering" the work
force when they encourage people to make their own decisions

about some aspect of their job. When someone has been assigned the right to make his or her own decisions, it is more appropriate to call this delegation. The term empowerment should be reserved for those situations where employees are *not* granted permission to take action on their own, but instead are asked to provide input to management as decisions are being made. You are empowered when you are valuable enough to others to influence their decisions—not when you are allowed to make your own.

Even if your suggestion is not implemented, you are empowered if your ideas are genuinely considered before the final decision is made. Empowered people do not always get what they want, but their input is always considered important and it carries weight with those making decisions.

Empowerment Is Not the Same as Courage
It is possible to act on one's convictions, but not be really influential with others. The act of offering someone your ideas or thoughts does not constitute empowerment unless you are considered valuable by that person. Therefore, empowerment represents both a person's willingness to provide input to decision makers and an environment where that input is valued.

When someone chooses to express his or her opinion despite the fact that the decision makers do not seek nor value such input, the act is referred to as courageous, not empowered. The students at Tiananmen Square were courageous, but they lacked the value to be influential with their governmental leaders. Therefore, they were not empowered.

Empowerment Is Not Synonymous with Autonomy
It is possible to be independent yet still be incapable of generating a desired result. To be empowered is to believe that you can significantly influence your own destiny. Empowered people do not think they control all the elements of their lives, but they do believe that, most of the time, they are responsible for a great deal of what happens to them.

In this context, responsibility implies neither blame nor acclaim, but rather the belief that most of the circumstances in which we find ourselves are the result of how we have defined the situations we face, the decisions we make, and the price we are willing to pay for what we want. So, the hallmarks of an empowered person are the creativity to frame the situation so success is possible, the capacity to face and make tough decisions, and the motivation to pay the price of success.

An empowered person has the creativity to define a situation in such a way that the likelihood of success improves. There are three different ways to define and approach situations.

1. *Opportunities:* Opportunities are potential benefits that require appropriate action to fully realize; opportunities can be exploited.

2. *Problems:* Problems have solutions. They may be elusive, but they can be prevented or resolved if you pay the price.

3. *Dilemmas:* Dilemmas have no solution. They are an inherent part of the situation at hand and, therefore, they must be accepted as inevitable. Sibling rivalry among young children is not a problem to be solved, but a dilemma to be managed.

Empowered people do not try to fix unresolvable problems; they learn instead how to live with the dilemma, or they shift from viewing a situation only as a problem to seeing the opportunities they might exploit. People spend their careers in one of two ways: (1) as victims of missed opportunities, unsolved problems, and unaccepted dilemmas, or (2) as architectural managers affecting these situations through their own creative actions.

The capacity to face and make tough decisions is the second essential component of empowerment. Either consciously or unconsciously, people are constantly making decisions that help determine the situations in which they later find themselves. For example, being unhappy in a marriage is, in part, the result of a prior decision regarding who to marry. Being successful in one's job is partially the result of a previous career decision. Since all decisions are made with insufficient data, once decisions are made, they can be sustained, modified, or reversed based on new information that is obtained over time. Sometimes, living an empowered life requires making tough decisions. The responsibility for what happens, or continues to happen, lies primarily with you.

The motivation to pay the price for success is a third key aspect of empowerment. Empowered people approach life as if it were an expensive pastime. They believe that people either pay dearly for getting what they want, or they pay dearly for not doing so. Since both invoices are expensive, they choose the one that represents the least cost for the most gain. They always know, however, that a price will be paid. How much is paid and what is received for that payment are the only options.

Although the organization must provide the appropriate environment, it also includes a self-concept earned through creative reframing, tough decisions, and expensive payments. This aspect of empowerment is not something that the organization grants employees and managers or transfers through training. Work environments can be established that attract empowered people and empowerment can be fostered, but it is not a quality that can be *given* to people simply because the organization has decided that it would be a good idea.

PARTICIPATIVE MANAGEMENT

The ability to operate synergistically requires more than empowered people; one must also be in an environment that fosters participation. Faced with continuous, overlapping change, many managers have come to realize the necessity for drawing on all their available resources as they deal with the constant state of flux. More managers have turned to participative management as a means of allowing people throughout their organizations to come to terms with the accelerated rate of change and the resulting new work environments.

A growing number of today's organizational tasks are too

complex for managers to totally control or implement effectively with ease. Managers must use all the resources at their disposal to bring about lasting organizational effectiveness. An organization's greatest resource for vital information, creative solutions, and timely support is its human resource—its employees.

Participative management is both a philosophy and a method for managing human resources in an environment in which employees are respected and their contributions valued and utilized. From a philosophical standpoint, participative management centers on the belief that people at all levels of an organization can develop a genuine interest in its success and can do more than merely perform their *assigned* duties. This approach involves employees in sharing information, solving problems, making decisions, planning projects, and evaluating results.

Although participative management encourages employee involvement in decisions affecting their work, this process can create problems if the nature of employee involvement is not clearly defined. Participative management should not be confused with consensus management. Inviting employee participation does not mean that management has relinquished its responsibility for final decisions. Management is instead *exercising* its responsibility by choosing to involve employees in reaching these decisions. Participative management is not an abdication of management control but a *form* of management control.

And yet, participative management maintains a balance of power. If you want employee input, you must deal with employees as if they had a true power base. Their power is in the value of their perspective and knowledge. If management and employees are in a true foxhole together, *both* seek the same thing and believe they need each other to accomplish the task.

Today's workers want more information relating to the overall direction and goals of the organization, more input concerning the objectives of their own work, and a greater value placed on their ideas about how this work can be accomplished more effectively. Management must remain ultimately responsible for all final decisions, but managers who use participative techniques make their decisions with a much broader input base.

If an organization wants to increase its effectiveness during change, everyone in the organization must demonstrate a high level of commitment toward the new initiatives. Organizational modifications can occur without commitment, but implementation will be difficult and costly in terms of lost production, absenteeism, turnover, alienation, and conflict. People are much more likely to support and take responsibility for projects they help create. Effectively using the participative approach will help produce the necessary commitment for successful change projects.

Managers who use participative techniques are not compelled to involve all their people in every decision all the time. Neither do all employees always have the same depth of involvement. Engaging employees in the change-related decisions affecting them is not a "yes" versus "no" decision. Participative management provides employees various degrees of involvement based on their familiarity with the task and the amount of flexibility for which the situation allows.

To summarize, the prerequisites for synergistic teamwork include the *willingness* to bring together diverse viewpoints to form a foxhole (accomplished by acknowledging common goals and interdependence) and the *ability* to demonstrate the appropriate skills for synergy to thrive (empowered people appropriately involved in participative methods to help manage the change process). Once a foxhole mentality generates the motivation to value diversity, and the empowerment and participative-management skills are in place, the process of synergy can unfold.

CHAPTER 12

THE SYNERGISTIC PROCESS

An organization's speed of change depends largely on how efficiently and effectively it advances through the four stages of synergy: interacting, appreciative understanding, integrating, and implementing.*

INTERACTION

Without interaction among team members, synergy cannot exist. If iron, carbon, and nickel are never brought together, the subsequent steps in the steel-manufacturing process are impossible. The same is true for people. For sponsors, agents, and targets to work together synergistically, they must first communicate effectively.

---

* The early framework for viewing synergy as a four-step process was developed by Henry Nelson Wieman in *Man's Ultimate Commitment,* published by The Foundation for Philosophy and Creativity, 1990.

If people working together have little or no opportunity for appropriate interaction, things degenerate quickly (see Figure 19 below). Normal misunderstandings go unresolved, and people become confused and angry. Frustrated, they then begin to blame each other (e.g., each party sees only positive characteristics in themselves while viewing only negative characteristics in the others). This tends to generate feelings of suspicion and alienation, which lead to further isolation. With the resulting increase in hostility, there is a decrease in the desire to interact with each

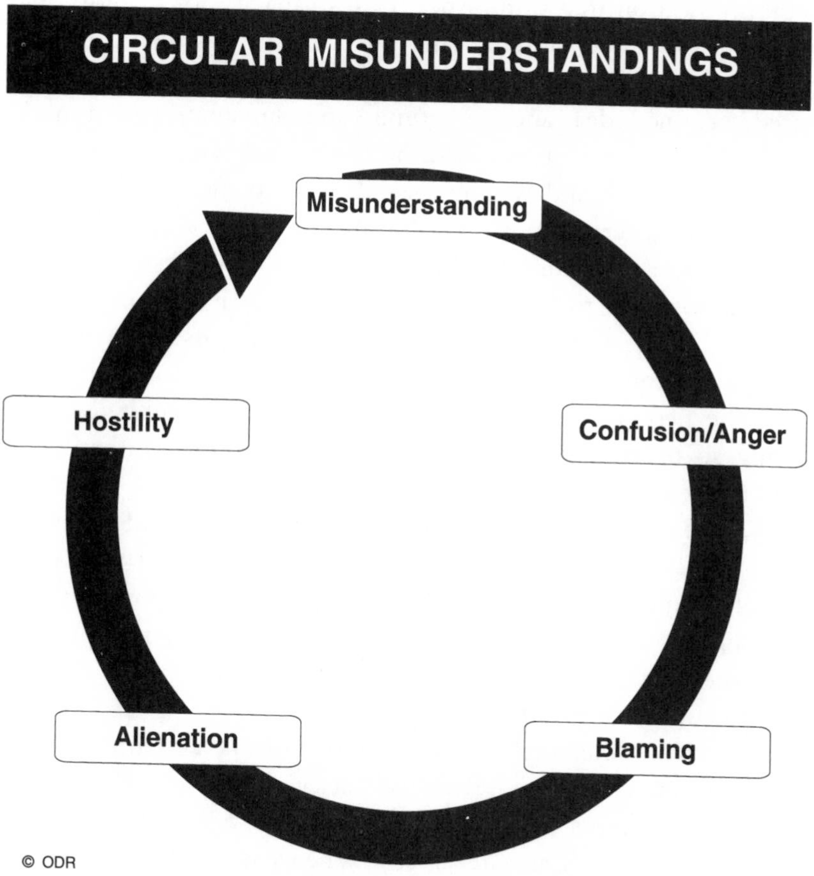

CIRCULAR MISUNDERSTANDINGS

Misunderstanding

Confusion/Anger

Hostility

Blaming

Alienation

© ODR

Figure 19

other. This lowers the possibility of correcting perceptual distortion, which breeds even deeper misunderstanding.

To avoid getting trapped in a self-destructive cycle of misunderstanding, implementation-team members must effectively communicate with each other. In this section, I will concentrate on three methods of interaction that guard against misunderstanding, confusion, blame, alienation, and hostility. They are: effective communication, active listening, and the production of an atmosphere of trust.

1. *Communicate effectively.* Common errors in interpersonal communication that diminish a team's capacity for synergy include using vague, obscure language; failing to perceive others' wants and needs; relying on unchecked assumptions; trusting predetermined ideas and stereotypes; and conveying verbal messages that are inconsistent with nonverbal behavior.

Both ability and willingness are vital to successfully completing the synergistic process. For example, a person may have the ability to communicate directly and with little distortion but may choose not to do so because she is worried about certain negative consequences of saying what she means. Likewise, a person or group may want desperately to communicate but may lack the necessary skills to do so or may be prohibited from doing so by organizational policies or procedures. Either case will block synergy.

2. *Listen actively.* There are three integral aspects of effective communication: the content of the message, the underlying values of the message, and the feelings people experience when they give and receive the message. Understanding the true meaning of messages conveyed between team members is a key goal of any synergistic work group.

Realizing the importance of fully hearing and processing information, synergistic teams use "active listening" skills (i.e., the listener accepts a major portion of the responsibility for the accuracy of the messages received). When you work with someone who employs active listening, you are generally more willing to participate and offer new thoughts, be more collaborative in dealing with others, be more loyal to the work group, and be more productive.

3. *Generate trust and credibility.* Trust among team members is absolutely essential; without it, people tend to respond with defensiveness, poor listening, indirectness, and high distortion. The trust I refer to is not the vague hope that your coworker is up to the challenge. It is also not the kind of trust based on simple good will and pleasantries (i.e., "I trust that they will not be rude or harsh in their dealings with us"). Synergistic trust is stronger, more fundamental. It is a trust based on mutual need, requisite skills, and a track record, not on hope or good will. "I strongly believe and, therefore, trust that you are in a foxhole with me, that we both are empowered and you will participate appropriately, and that you have a track record of getting the job done."

As essential as effective communication is for successful change, something more has to occur. Participants in a team effort must value and take advantage of their own diversity. For example, if a self-destructive relationship exists between a company's sales and production departments, you might assume all they need to do is learn to communicate better. But in many such situations, poor communication skills are not the true problem.

People involved in a sales-versus-production struggle often communicate well—so well, in fact, that they know exactly why they don't like each other. This happens when implementing organizational change as well. Sponsors and targets often communicate so clearly with each other that each group is convinced of the other's incompetence.

Synergy requires more than adequate communication. It demands true appreciative understanding—the capacity to value and use diversity. It is unlikely that you will ever learn to appreciate an opposing viewpoint if you insist on using only your own rational, linear, left-brain thinking processes. These approaches are dedicated to isolating events, separating right from wrong as seen from your perspective, and locating errors as you view the situation.

While the use of critical thinking is an important aspect of human perception, its overuse can be a weakness. You must achieve balance by merging opposing perspectives from two individuals or two groups into one viewpoint that is considered superior by all parties. Another way to achieve this balance is by looking for creative ways of making something work that wouldn't normally occur to your more linear left brain.

To achieve appreciative understanding, you must understand *why* others see something differently from you. You do not necessarily have to agree with them. If you announce a major corporate reorganization only to have someone say it is a terrible idea and won't work, you do not have to agree with him or her to foster synergy. You only have to see it from his or her viewpoint: "If I had just received this announcement and this was all the information that I had, I would probably feel the same way. I don't agree with this analysis, but I see how he arrived at it."

Agreement is not the key test for synergy; in fact, natural conflicts of diverse options are evidence that synergy is building. When people in a team relationship truly value their own diversity, they are not so threatened by each other. The foxhole in which they reside helps to keep them from pushing each other away.

The one soldier in the foxhole with the weapon appreciates the value of the other one who has the ammunition; one doesn't care about the other's cultural background, religion, or race. Organizationally, you enter the same circumstances when you can acknowledge the value of others, recognizing that they have the political ammunition to push your change project forward.

Another example: You may have previously disdained someone in your office because, although he has the necessary technical background, he doesn't have an MBA like you. Valuing diversity would mean that you would be thrilled that he does not have the same education and job skills as you. Suppose that you created a brilliant outline for a report, but he is the only one who can run the necessary analysis on the computer to generate the numbers for a badly needed chart. Management is looking to both of you to produce the necessary information quickly. Now you are in a foxhole together; if you recognize and utilize his unique skills, you will succeed with a complete report—better than anything either of you could have come up with on your own.

For implementation teams to be synergistic, there must be a balance between both the rational, critical-thinking process and the creative, merging process. There are four elements to achieving this balanced, appreciative understanding.

1. *Create an open climate.* Even when team members have interacted effectively and generated trust and credibility with each other, at some point they are going to disagree about certain aspects of the change. These inevitable differences can be handled properly if there is a commitment among team members to bring such issues to the surface and address them in a timely and direct manner. This requires the strong conviction that conflict is not inherently negative, but rather a normal and even positive occurrence.

Most people have been taught erroneously that the path to truth is through selection by exclusion (i.e., one reviews all the relevant data about a problem, rejecting that which does not fit his or her frame of reference). The process of stripping away possible solutions continues until a single answer remains. This is the basis of many change efforts.

For example, when seeking a solution to a change-related problem, sponsors, agents, and targets tend to reject the "obviously inappropriate" suggestions that each group offers the others. A mutually acceptable solution, if found at all, is the one that survived the gauntlet. Such an attitude toward joint problem solving consumes enough time and energy to ruin a company while the members run in circles.

Such a situation often produces a defensive, unpleasant climate in which people regard conflict as bad and something to avoid—even though the opposite is true (see Figure 20). If viewed as an ally, conflict can help clarify facts, stimulate new insights,

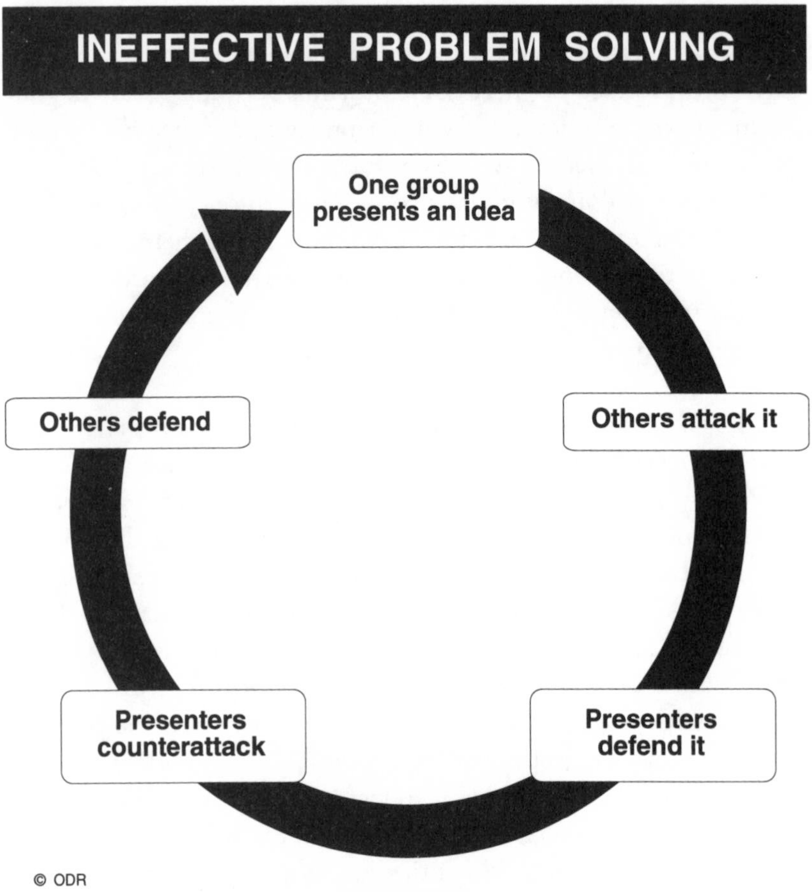

Figure 20

and lead to original solutions. By preventing the *win-lose* conflict climate and encouraging a *win-win* atmosphere, team members learn to be positive about conflict and realize that openly stating their differences helps to solve problems and take advantage of opportunities.

2. *Delay negative judgments.* To create appreciative understanding, sponsors, agents, and targets have to first feel free to express their thoughts and feelings about a change without fear of being attacked or told that their input is not valuable. This

means that everyone on the team must have the discipline to delay forming negative judgments about others' input.

Most innovative ideas or perspectives about a change are as vulnerable as newborn babies; they cannot survive unless someone takes responsibility for their protection and development. Attacking a new idea makes no more sense than saying of an infant: "Look at this child—he can't walk, he can't control his bodily functions. This kid is useless!"

Some new ideas are strong enough at birth to withstand the strain of critical analysis, but most will die without support. Since the core of synergy is diversity, you cannot afford to cultivate an environment in which only a few ideas survive the incubation stage.

Eventually, you have to address and overcome the shortcomings of innovative ideas or new perspectives regarding change. But if you delay the negative focus for a short while, an idea can survive to be further modified and developed.

3. *Empathize with others.* Empathizing with another person requires being both knowledgeable about what that person is experiencing and emotionally sensitive to the depth of that experience. Demonstrating empathy for another person's thoughts, feelings, and values, especially when that person expresses a viewpoint different from yours, is a powerful means for facilitating synergy within a work team.

Empathizing with each other's differing viewpoints does not require team members to always agree about how to implement the change. Empathy provides a vantage point from which each person can see the other's position. Among synergistic team members, you are unlikely to hear people describe those whom they disagree with as "stupid," "crazy," or "out in left field." The disagreements are passionate at times but never destructive—because hurting someone in your own foxhole means that you hurt yourself.

4. *Value diversity.* Valuing the diversity that exists in working relationships encourages team members to develop a strong sense of acceptance. People who feel accepted because their opin-

ions are valued usually contribute earnestly to a task. The affirmations team members receive from each other make them feel more valuable and influential. In the end, everyone is inclined to contribute even more.

It is here that sponsors need to be open to and positive about suggestions and feedback from agents and targets. The real challenge comes when such feedback is not consistent with what the sponsors perceive or want to be true. Synergy is enhanced any time team members' perspectives are expanded by the diversity offered through others. This is particularly true when the differences that surface represent a strong polarization of views.

A key outcome of synergy is that while working on a task, people generate and sustain resources rather than block or waste them. This effective use of resources does not appear magically. It results from the combined efforts of people working together cohesively and feeling understood, valued, influential, and trusted.

Too often when agents or targets offer ideas about how a change can be handled, the situation resembles a skeet shoot, with sponsors overtly attacking input or using a subtle, placating style of ignoring the objections that they hear. In this kind of environment, the only ideas that survive are the ones the sponsor fails to pulverize.

Synergistic teams reverse these roles. The responsibility for defending an idea rests with the receiver, not the originator. For example, when the targets' ideas are presented the sponsor will support the input and look for its best elements. Everyone is committed to identifying the positive aspects of a divergent perspective before finding fault. Such behavior generates a powerful, nurturing incubator for new ideas.

INTEGRATION

You can disagree strongly with someone and yet still foster empowerment. If you are a manager and acknowledge that you are in a foxhole situation with someone who works for you, that person knows that you cannot afford to write her off simply because you disagree. This gives her the confidence to state her disagreements, recognizing that because you need her to accomplish an important task, you are more likely to listen to her input. Knowing that you value diversity gives her the potential to influence your decision. This type of relationship is critical if divergent perspectives are to be integrated.

Merging diversity is a difficult process for many people because they have not been exposed to or rewarded for the skills needed for this type of integration. This part of the process is likely to run counter to many of the things people have been taught throughout their lives. There are four approaches winners use to successfully complete the integration process:

1. *Tolerate ambiguity and be persistent.* Integrating diverse views is most difficult for those who are only comfortable with quick, logical solutions. People tend to look for fast solutions when facing ambiguous circumstances. Writer and editor H. L. Mencken best addressed the flaw of relying on the easy way out by saying, "For every complex problem in the world, there exists a simple solution—which is almost always wrong."

The natural human desire for comfort leads people to opt sometimes for solutions they suspect may be unsuitable but are less ambiguous and more familiar. It is a corollary to the spray-and-pray approach; the desire for an answer is so strong that even faulty ones are appealing.

Resolution of the opportunities, problems, or dilemmas that result from change is not always a quick, clean-cut process. Your team may have to muddle its way through vague, contradictory, inaccurate, or misleading data concerning the change situation. Such ambiguity is rarely the result of sloppy data collection; it usually stems from the fact that most major change situations today are extraordinarily complex. Successful change implementation requires that you accept—and even value—the ambiguity of the situation until order can be structured from the chaos.

2. *Be pliable.* A problem endemic to integrating diversity is

the tendency we have to converge our ideas with those of other team members only as long as *they* are willing to be flexible. It is something else entirely when we are the ones required to budge.

For example, sponsors and agents often view targets as unsophisticated, uninformed, or unconcerned about overall organizational issues. This makes sponsors and agents unwilling to modify their change plans using the input from targets, who are perceived as mere underlings. Such an attitude is a death sentence to the fragile process of building synergistic working relationships.

In today's disjointed world, no one has or can have all the answers. Further, the knowledge gap between sponsors, agents, and targets is narrowing. Synergy can only occur when all members of an implementation team are willing to, and actually do, modify their views so they can be integrated with others.

3. *Be creative.* As team members attempt to integrate their diverse ideas into mutually supported action plans, creative thinking becomes a necessity.

Occasionally, varying input from sponsors, agents, and targets seems to fit together quickly. Other situations necessitate breaking out of established thought patterns. This requires a shift from linear or sequential logic-based thought to analogic-based thought, or what the creativity specialist Edward de Bono refers to in his 1971 book *Lateral Thinking* as moving from "vertical" to "lateral thinking."

> Logic is the tool that is used to dig holes deeper and bigger to make them altogether better holes. But if the hole is in the wrong place, then no amount of improvement is going to put it in the right place.
>
> No matter how obvious this may seem to every digger, it is still easier to go on digging in the same place than to start all over again in a new place. *Vertical thinking* is digging straight down, deeper into the same hole; *lateral thinking* is trying again elsewhere.

The successful melding of dissimilar viewpoints requires lateral, analogical thinking. Sponsors and agents—especially those in the highest positions within an organization—tend to believe that they arrived where they are because the hole is already in the right place. It seems logical to them to simply dig deeper in the place that has served them well before.

In spite of popular rhetoric to the contrary, creative problem solving is rarely rewarded in most American corporate settings. Instead, we tend to honor and promote strong-willed, fast-acting "logical" individuals to senior levels. An overabundance of linear or vertical thinking is a serious disadvantage for those seeking to achieve the synergy necessary to prosper in today's complex world.

4. *Be selective.* This is the cautionary element in the synergy process—the need for a balancing factor between tolerating ambiguity and being persistent. Deciding too early that a merger of ideas cannot or should not be pursued is dysfunctional—the breakthrough to integration often lies immediately beyond the team's last attempt. But when integration is hopeless, struggling to continue is a waste of resources.

Synergistic team members are balanced in their persistence and can stop or proceed, depending on the circumstances of each situation. Sometimes, diverse perspectives from sponsors, agents, and targets cannot be integrated, even after applying the steps previously described.

There is such a thing as a bad idea. If you come across one, don't integrate it—discard it. Taking a long-term, big-picture view while evaluating each member's input is always prudent.

At this point in the process, while disagreements may still remain, group members either pull together their disparate ideas or make a determination that such a blend is not possible. In the latter instance, the sponsor exercises his or her judgment about how to proceed. In any case, it is important to build a bridge across the chasm of disagreements before the group can implement action—the final phase of the synergistic process.

IMPLEMENTATION

Without a concrete payoff, no organization is going to spend valuable time fostering good working relationships. Achieving synergy can make change work, and the payoff is a successful business in an ever-changing world.

This final phase of the synergistic process harnesses the momentum generated thus far. The vital elements here are sound management practices—familiar territory for most people. What gets managed, however, is the human capacity to work as a team. Managing the energy unleashed through synergistic teamwork is as important as managing any other valuable resource. To successfully implement it, there are four approaches you must adopt:

1. *Strategize.* People working within synergistic relationships realize the value of planning action steps that are specific, measurable, and goal oriented. Without such direction, you could not manage resources, determine priorities, or ensure that individual activities are compatible.

Without a baseline to judge development, how can the effect of a change be verified? Production or delivery of services need to be measured before and after change implementation to monitor progress. Synergy is necessary to achieve challenging, but attainable, change goals. When reached, these goals establish standards for subsequent efforts.

2. *Monitor and reinforce.* When making their moves, synergistic implementation teams must be able to oversee progress and offer solutions to any problems that develop. Without disciplined follow-through, many otherwise sound plans fail. Lack of watchfulness during implementation rarely results from laziness, but from an error commonly made in human relations—the belief that once a common goal is announced, all parties will perceive that goal in the same way and feel the same urgency to achieve it.

We humans constantly modify our perceptions through our senses, perspectives, attitudes, and feelings regarding any event. This is especially true during change. New environmental factors will continually influence the individual team members' efforts toward goal achievement.

As important as it is, monitoring a change project is not enough. When progress or problems are identified, synergistic team members apply the correct consequences to ensure the implementation will succeed. To sustain your change, you must apply positive reinforcement for appropriate behavior and progress, as well as negative consequences for inappropriate behavior or lack of sufficient progress.

3. *Remain team focused.* Working as a synergistic team demands that the group remain sensitive to the needs of the individuals within the team, the team as a group, and the organization itself. As we discussed previously, it is not unusual to have sponsors, agents, and targets all perceive and respond differently to an impending change.

When such differences appear in nonsynergistic environments, individuals begin to operate at their own speed, knowledge, and competency level while decreasing their interaction with each other. Agents may begin to find it too frustrating to work with targets, so they develop plans on their own; this poisons the potential for the full value of synergy.

It may seem natural to you that those who are more competent at a task should move ahead faster than others. But that attitude fails to acknowledge that the change project had progressed as far as it has because of the project's original synergistic approach (i.e., sponsors, agents, and targets had all agreed earlier that they were in a foxhole together and could not succeed alone).

Honoring the original acknowledgment of common goals and interdependence means you must sacrifice the potential of some team members so that the total team can remain a unified, integrated work unit. For example, former Chicago Bear running back Walter Payton could run faster and make sharper cuts on the football field than any of his teammates. Yet his success was based on his ability to synchronize his moves with the support of his blockers.

Payton probably experienced countless situations in which

he could have cut to a different direction and run faster. But he knew that if he outran his blockers, he would simply have been left alone to meet opposing tacklers at a greater speed. You will rarely find a successful team-sport superstar who ignores the efforts of his or her teammates.

Similarly, your organization will not be best served if you slam into obstacles at your own maximum speed. You will score more touchdowns by moving through the openings that your teammates help clear for you.

4. *Update.* Unstable environments produce constantly changing variables. Reacting to these shifts in a manner that assists goal achievement requires a continuous updating of action plans. Sometimes people don't need to change; plans do.

Implementation teams often make the mistake of falling in love with their own plan. They transfer their egos to the project and perceive normal resistance to it as a personal attack. When this happens, they invest more energy in defending their plan than they do in working to achieve the task at hand. When resistance surfaces, a synergistic team applauds the open dialogue and redesigns the plan as necessary.

DEVELOPING SYNERGY

There are five basic skills that help foster synergy. You must:

1. *Establish prerequisites.* Build the motivation (common goals and interdependence) and abilities (empowerment and participative management) that are the foundation for synergy.
2. *Support permeability.* Help people express and be open to learning new ideas, perspectives, meanings, values, feelings, behaviors, and attitudes they would not otherwise accept or exchange.
3. *Encourage paradoxical thinking.* Help people live through the frustration and confusion that occurs when they

attempt to merge apparently contradictory ideas, view-points, feelings, or attitudes.

4. *Facilitate creativity.* Teach people to value the integration of opposing views, causing a shift from "either/or" opposing relationships to "both/and" supportive relationships.

5. *Structure discipline.* Use the new, mutually supported concepts to pursue specific objectives, assign task responsibility, and stick to schedule until the change is fully accomplished.

In my years of observing people all over the world as they have attempted to work together in facing change, I have seen strong, sustained synergy take place only when the people involved believed the price for not functioning this way was prohibitively high. Synergy requires an enormous price, yet its absence can cost even more. Empowered people who share a fox-hole must involve each other appropriately as they communicate their diversity, value what each other has to say, and integrate these ideas before action is taken. As expensive as such a process is, it is also an extremely powerful mechanism for increasing an organization's resilience and speed of absorbing change.

THE THREE KEY PRINCIPLES IN THE "SYNERGY AND CHANGE" PATTERN

When involved in major organizational change, you can enhance resilience if you:

1. Recognize how important synergy is to the success of change.

2. Are willing (common goals and interdependence) and able (empowerment and participation) to join with others in efforts that produce a $1 + 1 > 2$ equation.

3. Can listen to, value, integrate with, and apply perspectives different from your own.

Part V

THE NATURE
OF RESILIENCE

*I*f you learn and use the dynamics of change to foster personal, organizational, and social resilience, you will survive and prosper during times of great change. In Parts III and IV, I identified key principles from the seven support patterns that are essential to increasing resilience. In Part V, the mechanisms of the eighth and primary pattern—resilience itself—become the focus. Throughout this section, my discussion will center on the previous definition of winners—those individuals and groups who are resilient, *who have the ability to absorb high levels of change while displaying minimal dysfunctional behavior.*

In the next three chapters, I will pursue the nature of resilience, the intuitive manner by which most people acquire it, and how to foster its development.*

---

* These chapters exclude one important aspect of resilience: the individual's physiological capacity. This exclusion is not intended to downplay the significance of health and wellness in achieving optimal resilience. I chose not to include the physiological factor in this context, due to the vast amount of information already available in medical books and journals concerning the physiological aspects of resilience. This information, however, should be taken into consideration in any exhaustive study of the subject.

CHAPTER 13

UNSEEN MECHANISMS

*B*y unveiling the hidden influences on our behavior during transitions we can become architects, instead of victims, of change. Two different types of people help demonstrate the dramatic role unseen mechanisms play in shaping a person's or an organization's ability to display resilience to change. Unconsciously incompetent people do not implement change effectively in their own lives nor orchestrate it well with others, and they do not know why. These people not only lack resilience, but are unaware of its very existence. In other words, they don't know that they don't know.

From a research standpoint, this group's behavior is extremely interesting: Their change-related failures are often spectacular; therefore, they provide excellent opportunities for cataloging what not to do. When unconsciously incompetent people confront major change, they are usually unable to make the necessary adjustments without displaying dysfunctional behavior. Either they never achieve their change objectives or do so only after expending a great deal more time and money than originally planned.

From my observations, the majority of senior managers who face the inevitable resistance of major change are unconsciously incompetent. They do not know how to guide their people through the change process, and they don't even recognize this deficiency or its effect on their organization's ability to function in perilous times.

The second category is the unconsciously competent. These are resilient people who tend to do the right things to successfully implement change but do not know what those things are or how they do them. They sometimes achieve their change objectives on time and within budget, but they cannot articulate the process that they use, and are seldom able to report exactly how they have become so effective at implementing change.

After years of observing and talking to such people all over the world, we realized that they were not simply "lucky," as many of them thought. They were following specific (though unconscious) guidelines that they had intuitively developed as a result of trial and error. These people were never novices at change. They were always heavily scarred from and therefore prepared by many encounters with future shock. That they were not consciously aware of the process they used to accommodate change in no way inhibited their success when they did apply this process. Nevertheless, because they were not following a conscious discipline, their methods were not always consistently applied.

Herein lies the first of two problems that plague the unconsciously competent. While they are often extremely successful in their execution of change, they also have the capacity to fail miserably. These people can work wonders in some change situations only to fall flat on their faces in others. Without awareness of the behavior that leads to success, it is virtually impossible to reproduce that success consistently. We have concluded that the proficiency these people demonstrate at implementing change

depends mostly on whether or not they are having a good day at
following their hunches—not exactly the most dependable system on which to rely when dealing with important changes.

The second and greater problem we've discovered is that
since they cannot relate to their skills as a conscious discipline,
they have a great deal of difficulty transferring their talents to
others.

Relying on unconscious competence makes it problematic to
teach resilience and change-management skills to others. It also
lends an air of mystery to the implementation process itself.
These individuals are often thought of as gurus inside their companies because they're the only ones who know the "magic."
Being a solo change guru in your company may do wonders for
your ego, but it generates a dangerous situation for any organization facing long-term major change.

The aftermath of the Persian Gulf War is an example of the
importance of being able to transfer a skill to others. Shortly after
Operation Desert Storm, Red Adair, the world's most famous
oil-well fire-fighting specialist, and his company were among the
few with the technical skills and experience to begin putting out
all the fires that Saddam Hussein's army had sparked in the Kuwaiti oil fields. The task was massive. The number of fires sur-
passed the combined total of all the oil-well fires in the world
since 1910. Adair announced that considering how few trained
personnel were available and the number and complexity of the
fires, the job would take at least five years to complete.

That was economically and environmentally unacceptable to
the Kuwaiti government. So Adair and his men began to train
other teams from various other countries. By the time they put
out the last fire, they had trained ten fire-fighting teams from
twenty-eight countries. Their combined effort finished the job in
less than a year.

There was never a suggestion on anyone's part that these
rookie fire fighters had acquired in a short time the same proficiency as that of Adair's master crew. But Adair was able to
transfer the basics of oil-well fire-fighting procedures and tech-

niques so that the various other crews could perform essential tasks and contribute to the overall effort.

The era is long past when one or two gurus can manage the changes being faced by most organizations. Even if you are fortunate enough to have a full complement of senior officers armed with intuitive change-management skills, your organization is still vulnerable. With today's complex markets and sophisticated change projects, you need cadres of skilled sponsors, agents, targets, and advocates within your organization who can respond to the ever-growing challenges that lie ahead.

Type-O attributes must become an essential part of leadership at every level, from the CEO to the line supervisor. We need executives and supervisors who are resilient and who know how to manage change in a consciously competent manner. They must successfully implement change for themselves and others, consistently apply the mechanisms they use, and be able to relate to these methods as a structured discipline so others can learn and apply the same skills.

LEARNING THE RHYTHM OF CHANGE

Prior to the invention of the thermometer and barometer in the seventeenth century, farmers all over the world operated without the advantage of even rudimentary scientific weather forecasting. They conducted their agricultural business in an environment in which unexplained, calamitous weather events could strike with no warning.

Without the benefit of forecasting information and a knowledge of how weather patterns formed, the early farmers were constantly surprised. They were grateful when good weather prevailed and felt victimized when it was bad—but they were always surprised. Worse, since they did not understand the forces they were up against, they were surprised at their surprise.

The modern manager faces a similar situation. Attempting to implement a major transition without understanding the human dynamics of change is like the early farmer waiting to see if the coming weeks would bring drought, rain, or a hurricane. In such situations, the farmer, like the untrained manager, has only hope and good intentions on his or her side. Armed with no more than this, a manager's chances of successfully implementing a change drop dramatically as the environment operates at a quickening pace and becomes increasingly complex and unpredictable. To the untrained executive, it seems just as impossible to anticipate and prepare for how people will respond to a change as it was for the agrarians of past ages to predict the weather.

When people are constantly surprised by unforeseeable, inexplicable events, they find it difficult to plan and manage their resources. Not until predicting the weather became a discipline—with scientific instruments and a process for predicting weather patterns with some degree of confidence—could modern farming develop. Today's farmers cannot control the climate, but they can anticipate weather-related events more accurately and manage their resources accordingly. In a similar manner, by applying knowledge of the typical behavior patterns humans display during change, today's executives can better predict the outcome of their efforts.

When people learn the rhythm of change, they can better mobilize their resources to increase their assimilation capacity and raise their future shock threshold. *It can be done!* The findings described here are not based on some new theory of change management. They are based on what we have learned from nearly twenty years of actually observing people as they participate in transformational change. I am convinced that resilience can be enhanced, because I have witnessed its development in people as they faced major change for which they were previously unprepared.

You can learn to discipline yourself to use the forces of change to your advantage—like learning to turn into a skid rather than succumbing to the natural tendency to turn away from it when driving on an icy road. Because it is so frightening, you probably won't ever look forward to disruptive change. But with increased resilience, you will be better prepared to respond with skill and confidence when transition occurs.

Remember, learning to understand human behavior does not mean you are immune to its consequences. Life and its inevitable changes will still surprise you. The advantage of greater resilience is that you will not be so surprised that you are surprised and, therefore, you will be in a better position to recover more quickly and effectively.

TEACHING RESILIENCE

Many people view change as prehistoric man viewed fire—that is, as an unsolvable mystery. People who think this way are limited to hoping that if they are lucky they will be blessed with the strength to survive and prosper during major transitions.

Is the amazing exhibition of resilience put on by Earvin "Magic" Johnson an example of qualities only the lucky can display? His strength and courage during his retirement from the NBA were a powerful source of inspiration at many levels. First is in the depth of character he demonstrated by dealing with his own fears and anxiety through promoting AIDS awareness for others.

Second, the realistic yet positive mental attitude he showed toward his circumstances enlightened many, showing them that there is an alternative to the victimization commonly felt in such situations. Being empowered is refusing to feel trapped with no options, regardless of what has happened. Magic Johnson demonstrated to all of us that even when facing our own mortality, there are potent actions we can take.

The role model Magic Johnson has provided us by taking this empowered approach to adversity far exceeds anything he could have accomplished on the basketball court. Millions of people around the world have been personally touched and significantly influenced by his actions. Most of these people would have previously thought of him as only a phenomenal athlete or a celebrity endorser of products on television. Now he has become an inspirational champion who transcends the limitations of a mere professional sports star.

Unfortunately, for many people his actions are to be admired but not emulated. To them, he is a role model for what could be possible for someone fortunate enough to be blessed with his inner strength, but as far as they are concerned his level of resilience isn't possible for themselves. Their esteem for his performance during change will not, in all likelihood, convince them that they can find this same capacity within themselves.

In part, their respect does not lead them to view him as a true mentor because they cannot see the skill behind his resilience as clearly as they could see his ball-handling dexterity for the Los Angeles Lakers. When desired behavior is recognizable, it can be searched out, identified, isolated, and studied. Aspiring high school basketball players can help enhance their ball-handling skills by watching videos of Johnson performing his magic on the court. By recognizing and studying his technique and practicing diligently, the young players can incorporate their version of his moves into their own game.

The same is true for watching Johnson's display of resilience. To gain full value from observing what he is doing with his life as he faces the implications of being HIV positive, we must recognize the basic structure of his resilience. We must demystify his resilience magic, isolate and study his moves if we are to be better equipped to replicate them.

As parents, executives, politicians, and citizens, we must all learn to be better prepared to manage our change resources by demystifying the dynamics of resilience, and learning to understand how it functions in order to emulate the actions of role models like Magic Johnson.

The Lamaze method of natural childbirth provides a good example of the value of uncovering the unseen structures that govern our response to change. My wife, Michaelene, and I took the Lamaze course prior to the birth of our son Chase. We learned about the different stages of labor so we both could understand what was happening. The classes enabled us to be more knowl-edgeable about when and why things would happen during labor and how to use methods such as breathing techniques to help manage the process.

Often the worst part of a painful experience is the fear of the unknown. The Lamaze techniques did not reduce Michaelene's physical pain during childbirth, but they did help prepare both of us for what was to come and enable us to be more resilient throughout the birth process. Classes like these provide basic information to let a couple expecting a child know what to an-ticipate. This knowledge allowed Michaelene to accommodate the pain, although it didn't lessen the severity. She did learn how to avoid the additional and unnecessary pain that occurs when a woman fights the natural process of childbirth. The class also enabled her to meet other expectant mothers and discover that her fears and concerns were similar and therefore completely normal.

It is possible to help people learn type-O attributes and in-crease their number of available assimilation points. By being better equipped to manage the transition process, leaders can increase their capacity and that of others to absorb change. With proper education and practice, major changes can be accom-plished while drawing a minimum of points from our assimila-tion accounts.

When people are preparing themselves for change, the key issues are "What will happen?" "When?" and "How will it affect me?" Answering these questions decreases ambiguity, reduces anxiety, and restores a measure of control—although the pain of the transition will still exist. As we discussed earlier, people have such a deep need for control that being able to anticipate and understand even a negative change can be regarded as a source of comfort.

You can consciously accelerate your speed of absorbing change and that of others by learning to use the elements within the structure of change to your advantage. In fact, learning to apply the implications from both the patterns in organizational change as well as their related resilience principles has become a key component of leadership. If you want to lead successful change, you must anticipate such things as:

- how and when people will react to a change;
- how they will express their resistance;
- how much commitment is needed to succeed;
- how this level of commitment can be attained; and
- how the family, organization, or societal culture will influence the final outcome.

With today's high stakes and fast pace, it is not good enough for resilience to manifest itself only through unconscious competence. With change being so critical to micro, organizational, and macro success, high levels of resilience are necessary at all three levels. The world needs more resilient people who are able to teach others how to accommodate change and travel successfully through their lives at an increasing rate of assimilation.

If you suspect your skills for being resilient place you in the unconsciously incompetent category, the following chapters should provide some helpful guidance. If you believe you are among the unconsciously competent, you will probably find this section of the book reinforcing. Here, you will find encouragement and a structure for consciously applying what you are already doing intuitively.

CHAPTER 14

RESPONDING TO THE CRISIS
OF CHANGE

*P*eople have found the concept of resilience intriguing for centuries. The ancient Greeks realized that to acquire resilience, you
had to possess what they termed "practical intelligence," which
in turn comes from valuing adaptability and believing that preparation and choice allow us to influence our future. The Greeks
also felt it was dangerous to assume that plans would ever fully
materialize as intended. Approaching life in this manner, they
believed, made people better prepared to address change.

The nimbleness and heartiness that resilient people show in
the face of adversity result from an elasticity that allows them to
remain relatively calm in unpredictable environments; they can
spring back repeatedly after being subjected to the stresses of
change. In fact, when resilient people face the ambiguity, anxiety,
and loss of control that accompany major change, they tend to
grow stronger from their experiences rather than feel depleted by
them.

Resilient people experience the same fear and apprehension
as everyone else when they engage change. However, they are

usually able to maintain their productivity and quality standards as well as their physical and emotional stability while achieving most of their objectives.

There are at least two things resilient people do that appear to reduce their susceptibility to dysfunctional behavior during change: increase the number of assimilation points they have available, thus raising their future shock threshold, and minimize the number of assimilation points needed for the successful implementation of any one change.

Increasing Available Assimilation Points

Resilient people are not satisfied with the hypothetical six hundred assimilation point limit discussed in Chapter 5. They engage in activity to move their threshold to eight hundred, one thousand, or fifteen hundred points and beyond. Since continuous quality improvement never stops, resilient people cannot be satisfied with a static assimilation capacity; they feel that next year will produce even more change demands with the assimilation ante going up yet again. Resilient managers continuously look for ways to help their people better absorb change by teaching them its dynamics and what they can do to manage the process. In this way, they actually increase the threshold at which they, and others, face the symptoms of future shock.

Decreasing Assimilation Points Used

Resilient people also minimize the number of assimilation points that they use to execute change. For example, if you anticipate resistance to a specific change and plan how to preempt or prepare for it, you and the people affected will consume fewer assimilation points.

While a certain number of points are required to absorb the implications of any major change, an equal or greater number of points are often consumed due to such things as ignorance of how people change, poor planning, inept communications, and mismanaged resistance. Resilient people minimize unnecessary consumption of assimilation points—both for themselves and others.

The combination of increasing the number of available assimilation points while reducing the number used on any one change project thwarts future shock. This yields a dramatic competitive advantage: the resilience to continuously adapt to shifting circumstances (see Figure 21).

CRISIS OR OPPORTUNITY?

ODR's research to date suggests that the presence of resilience is not a characteristic that either does or does not occur in individuals. Resilience is a combination of traits that is manifested to

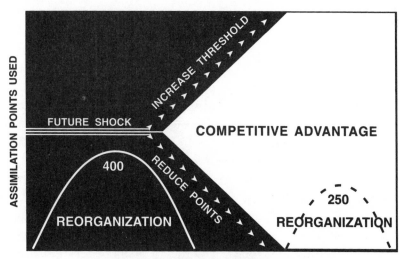

THE COMPETITIVE ADVANTAGE OF RESILIENCE

© ODR

Figure 21

various extents in different people. To understand the different degrees of resilience, it is helpful to view people as having a preference toward one of two orientations to change.

Change produces a crisis when it significantly disrupts our expectations about important issues or events. The Chinese express the concept of crisis with two separate symbols. The top character represents potential danger, the lower one conveys hidden opportunity. By combining these two symbols, the Chinese seem to be characterizing change as a paradox.

In observing how people respond to the stress produced by the crisis of change, our research found two common orientations, each with a particular perspective on the crises induced by change. While one tends to see primarily dangerous implications, the other typically focuses on the promise of new opportunities. Let's use the Chinese symbols as a reference point in describing the orientation of the two groups we identified.

DANGER-ORIENTED PEOPLE

Danger-oriented, or type-D, people view the crisis of change as threatening and can feel victimized by it. Such people often lack an overarching sense of purpose or vision for their lives, and therefore, they often find it difficult to reorient themselves when the unanticipated disrupts their expectations.

They tend to interpret life in binary and sequential terms, thinking that change should progress in a logical and orderly fashion. Since the world rarely offers major change in such a simple package, a type-D person's tolerance for ambiguity is usually not fully developed. For them, change is an unnatural, unnecessary, and unpleasant departure from the comforting stability of the status quo.

During periods of unrest, danger-oriented people typically feel insecure about themselves and their ability to manage uncertainty. They are unaware of the dynamics of human change, often feeling the need to defend themselves against what appear to be mysterious, random emotional reactions that they and others sometimes have when facing disruption. They also are often reluctant to acknowledge the need for change. Some of the more common defense mechanisms they use are:

- *Denial:* "I don't see anything that would suggest an alteration in our planned course."
- *Distortion:* "Well, the information does not look that bad to me."
- *Delusion:* "All this high-tech talk is nothing but hot air. We don't have to worry; no computer can do our jobs."

When faced with change, type-D people generally respond in a reactive, rather than a proactive, fashion. They tend to avoid the forces of change in themselves and others as long as possible. When a major change can no longer be ignored, they have too little time to plan an appropriate response strategy. Since the need to change is invariably acknowledged late, they are left with only their knee-jerk reactions to defend themselves, or their families, organizations, industries, or countries.

Last-minute reactions to change are usually ineffective. But I actually believe that D-type personalities would be only slightly more effective if they took the time to plan for change. They simply lack the knowledge and skill to accurately anticipate the need for change, diagnose the potential resistance problems, design a plan of action, and manage the implementation process.

To avoid their fear of change and lack of knowledge about what to do, D types often react to a significant disruption in their expectations by throwing up smoke screens. For example, sometimes they interpret unexpected change as the result of personal vendettas or conspiracies. "Of course they closed my office! They knew if I had three more months to hit my numbers that I could prove I was right and they were wrong about my approach."

Other times they may try to shift the focus of attention to someone else: "If only Jones had done his job, we wouldn't be in this mess."

Regardless of the mechanisms used, type-D people often blame and attack someone or something for the problems caused by change. This behavior not only inhibits problem solving and demoralizes others, but it is also counterproductive. Blaming and attacking only result in counterblaming and counterattacking by others. The energy that should be devoted to addressing the change is instead diverted to face-saving and CYA (cover your ass) activities, usually resulting in increased anxiety and hostility.

In the past, the rate of change was of a magnitude that better accommodated type-D people. Changes were more isolated and evolutionary in nature; thus, the impact was less disruptive and easier to contend with. In today's chaotic environment, these people, with increasing frequency, experience gaping holes in their defenses against the stress, ambiguity, conflict, and disequilibrium brought on by change.

As the reality of change crashes in on them, they feel more and more overwhelmed and incapable in a world they perceive as unpredictable, confusing, and contradictory. They see that their responses to events and issues are no longer adequate. They apply all the skill and knowledge that may have brought success in the past, but that now tend to yield failure, humiliation, and defeat.

A type-D response to the crisis of change has less to do with a person's age than with issues such as his or her perspective on change or available resources to assimilate the change. So the type-D approach to change is by no means limited to older individuals or the soon to retire. Because the need to train people in change tactics and resilience strategies is not recognized as part of a required core curriculum by most public schools, colleges, graduate schools, or management-training programs, many young people today demonstrate type-D characteristics. Even more problematic is that most parents place more emphasis on competitive sports than they do on cultivating the resilience capabilities of their children.

The type-D orientation toward change is not found only in individuals. You will also see it in family relations, group dynamics, church politics, management teams, organizational cultures, community relations, industry attitudes, and national biases. This sort of mentality can dramatically inhibit your ability to manage transitions for yourselves and others at the optimum speed of change.

OPPORTUNITY-ORIENTED PEOPLE

The opportunity-oriented, or type-O, response to the crisis of change is dramatically different. While recognizing the dangers, it positions change as a potential advantage to be exploited, rather than a problem to be avoided.

Type-O people usually have a strong life vision that serves as a source of meaning and as a beacon guiding them through the turmoil and adversity of change. When the unanticipated throws them off course, they are able to regain their bearings by realigning their sense of purpose. This purpose may be expressed by their religious beliefs, their political convictions, a philosophy toward life, or a compelling task they are trying to accomplish during their lifetime. Whatever its manifestations, this vision functions as a template that they lay on top of the ambiguities that arise as they strive to stay on their charted course.

Type-O people view life as a set of constantly shifting, interacting variables that produce an escalating number of combinations. Each day, type-O people assume that tomorrow will spawn a new set of opportunities and choices that will produce even more demanding challenges.

When disruption occurs, this group experiences the same feeling of disorientation as type-D people, but type-O people feel less of a need to defend themselves against such feelings. They view disruption and its accompanying discomforts as a necessary (if unpleasant) part of the adjustment process. They invest in developing various mechanisms to manage these inevitable disruptions rather than waste their resources avoiding them.

For example, a type-O person tends to compartmentalize the stress caused by disruptions and, in doing so, is able to contain the strain of change that she may be feeling in one area of her life, and prevent it from causing disruptions in another. Such a person would isolate the anger and frustration she feels toward a particular group in the office and resist transferring these emotions to other work groups during the day or family members in the evening. Not only does this prevent the inappropriate release of these emotions to unsuspecting associates and loved ones, but it helps the individuals as well. Such behavior allows the type-O person to avoid the drain on resources that would result from escalating problems in other areas of her life.

Type-O people also protect their assimilation capacity by not engaging in change efforts that require resources they don't possess. They know the limitations of their personal and organizational resources, and refuse to waste their time, money, and energy pursuing change initiatives that cannot be successfully supported. Though they are cautious about overextending themselves, they also tend to be creative about how to maximize the use of their resources. They are constantly challenging their own assumptions and frames of reference about how something can be accomplished.

A related aspect of how type-O people operate is that they recognize when to ask for help. These people are often independent and self-sufficient, yet they know when to tap the special skills of those around them in order to achieve common change goals. In this way, they conserve their own assimilation capacity and liberate new team resources to absorb change.

Another mechanism that type-O people tend to use to bounce back from the strain of change is their reliance on nurturing relationships. Such relationships provide a safe haven where love and acceptance are available to rejuvenate energy and regain perspective. For some people, this nurturing is provided by their family or close friends, and for others it is secured through religious organizations or support groups.

A salient characteristic of type-O people is their acceptance of change as a natural part of life. Type-D people don't even expect significant change and, therefore, they suffer a shock when established realities suddenly shift.

The type-O group is spared some of the shock's intensity because change does not shatter their presumptions; they never assume that their world will remain unchanged. They view change, even major, unanticipated change, as a natural part of human experience. It is seen as a challenge replete with problems to solve and opportunities to exploit, rather than something terrifying to avoid. Type-O people are not surprised by life's inevitable changes.

Type-O people also do not anticipate that life will unfold in a logical, easily rationalized manner with clear-cut, right-or-wrong options. Instead, they expect to be confronted with confusing, mixed signals which must be deciphered and acted upon. They are better equipped to deal with these kinds of situations because they are prepared to see the paradox that so often lies below the surface of what appears to be a situation filled with contradiction.

Type-O people have an ability to achieve balance in their perspective. They see such things as opportunities hidden within dangers, the humor of serious situations, the order embedded in chaos, the patience necessary in urgent circumstances, the alterations necessary for things to remain the same, the constancy that exists within a transition, and the fact that even as people strive toward perfection they must accept its impossibility.

The type-O ability to respond in a constructive and positive way to transition does not occur because of any special immunity to the problems associated with change. When faced with disruptive change, these people are as vulnerable to the discomforts of confusion, anxiety, and stress as type-D people. The main difference between the two groups is not the feelings of discomfort generated by change—both have these emotions. It is their *reactions* to these feelings that differ.

While type-D individuals tend to become immobilized and

react with fear, denial, or complacency, type-O people recognize the discomfort as a signal to activate their coping mechanisms and adapt to the shifting circumstances.

Type-O people are therefore quicker to determine that a change is inevitable, necessary, or advantageous. They engage their coping mechanisms faster when old frames of reference no longer appear relevant, and move to a problem-solving mode. Instead of blaming others for the unexpected, they incorporate what they have learned from the disruption into new frames of reference, which lead them to a fresh understanding of the situation.

As solutions are generated, stability and productivity are regained. Of course, it is only a matter of time until the disruption of change once again alters expectations and the process begins again.

THE FIVE BASIC CHARACTERISTICS OF RESILIENCE

The general descriptions provided above regarding type-O people can be organized into categories that reflect five basic characteristics of resilience. Type-O, resilient people:

1. Display a sense of security and self-assurance that is based on their view of life as complex but filled with opportunity (Positive);
2. Have a clear vision of what they want to achieve (Focused);
3. Demonstrate a special pliability when responding to uncertainty (Flexible);
4. Develop structured approaches to managing ambiguity (Organized);
5. Engage change rather than defend against it (Proactive).

Resilient people are: positive, focused, flexible, organized, and proactive. These five basic characteristics of resilience are manifested by certain beliefs, behaviors, skills, and areas of knowledge. Listed below are the attributes that are most noteworthy for each characteristic.

Attributes

Positive—Views Life as Challenging but Opportunity Filled

- Interprets the world as multifaceted and overlapping
- Expects the future to be filled with constantly shifting variables
- Views disruptions as the natural result of a changing world
- Sees life as filled with more paradoxes than contradictions
- Sees major change as uncomfortable, but believes that hidden opportunities may usually exist
- Believes there are usually important lessons to be learned from challenges
- Sees life as generally rewarding

Focused—Clear Vision of What Is to Be Achieved

- Maintains a strong vision that serves both as a source of purpose and as a guidance system to reestablish perspectives following significant disruption

Flexible—Pliable When Responding to Uncertainty

- Believes change is a manageable process
- Has a high tolerance for ambiguity
- Needs only a short time to recover from adversity or disappointment
- Feels empowered during change
- Recognizes one's own strengths and weaknesses and knows when to accept internal or external limits
- Challenges and, when necessary, modifies one's own assumptions or frames of reference
- Relies on nurturing relationships for support
- Displays patience, understanding, and humor when dealing with change

Organized—Applies Structures to Help Manage Ambiguity

- Identifies the underlying themes embedded in confusing situations
- Consolidates what appear to be several unrelated change projects into a single effort with a central theme
- Sets and, when necessary, renegotiates priorities during change
- Manages many simultaneous tasks and demands successfully
- Compartmentalizes stress in one area so that it does not carry over to other projects or parts of one's life
- Recognizes when to ask others for help
- Engages major action only after careful planning

Proactive—Engages Change Instead of Evading It

- Determines when a change is inevitable, necessary, or advantageous
- Uses resources to creatively reframe a changing situation, improvise new approaches, and maneuver to gain an advantage
- Takes risks despite potentially negative consequences
- Draws important lessons from change-related experiences that are then applied to similar situations
- Responds to disruption by investing energy in problem solving and teamwork
- Influences others and resolves conflicts

THE RESILIENCE CONTINUUM

The ongoing ODR investigation of resilience has found no one person or group who was purely D type or O type. It was found, however, that when faced with significant change, the majority of people will most often respond according to a preferred orientation. Think of D types and O types as representing the extremes of a resilience continuum. People move from side to side on the continuum all the time, yet D types clearly show a preference for one end of the scale, while O types tend to gravitate toward the other end. From this perspective I offer the following continuum.

RESILIENCE CONTINUUM

Low ← ――――――――――――――――――――――→ High

D TYPE	O TYPE
Positive	
Interprets the world as binary and sequential.	Interprets the world as multifaceted and overlapping.
Expects future to be orderly and predictable.	Expects future to be filled with constantly shifting variables.
Interprets unmet expectations as personal vendettas or conspiracies.	Views disruptions as the natural result of a changing world.
Spends time resolving many contradictions.	Spends time understanding many paradoxes.
Sees major change as uncomfortable and a problem to avoid.	Also sees major change as uncomfortable but views it as often presenting opportunities to exploit.
Feels that most challenges are unfair and serve no purpose.	Believes there are usually lessons to be learned from challenges.
Sees life as generally punishing.	Sees life as generally rewarding.
Focused	
Lacks an overarching purpose or vision and/or the ability to stay focused on its achievement.	Maintains a strong purpose or vision that serves both as a source of meaning and as a guidance system to reestablish perspectives following significant disruption.

Low ←————————————————→ High

D TYPE   **O TYPE**

Flexible

D TYPE	O TYPE
Approaches change as a mysterious event.	Believes change is a manageable process.
Has a low tolerance for ambiguity as evidenced by poor performance in unstructured or uncertain work environments.	Has a high tolerance for ambiguity.
Needs a long recovery time after adversity or disappointment.	Needs only a short time to recover after adversity or disappointment.
Feels victimized during change.	Feels empowered during change.
Engages in changes that are beyond personal or organizational capabilities.	Recognizes one's own strengths and weaknesses and knows when to accept internal or external limits.
Fails to break from established way of seeing things.	Challenges and when necessary modifies one's own assumptions or frames of reference.
Does not develop and maintain nurturing relationships that can be used for support.	Relies on nurturing relationships for support.
Lacks patience, understanding, and humor in the face of change.	Displays patience, understanding, and humor when dealing with change.

Organized

D TYPE	O TYPE
Becomes lost when faced with confusing information.	Identifies the underlying themes embedded in confusing situations.

Low ⟵⟶ High

D TYPE	O TYPE
Engages in too many diverse change projects that collectively drain assimilation resources.	Consolidates what appear to be several unrelated change projects into a single effort with a central theme.
Cannot establish and/or update priorities during change.	Sets and renegotiates priorities during change.
Fails to effectively manage multiple tasks and demands that occur at the same time.	Manages many simultaneous tasks and demands successfully.
Cannot compartmentalize tasks and pressures, so one stress point spills over into other areas.	Skilled at compartmentalizing so that stress in one area does not carry over to other projects or parts of one's life.
Fails to ask others for help when it is needed.	Recognizes when to ask others for help.
Is prone to knee-jerk reactions.	Engages action only after careful planning.

Proactive

Unable to recognize impending or potential change situations.	Determines when a change is inevitable, necessary, or advantageous.
Rigidly adheres to old operating style when facing the unexpected.	Reframes changing situations, improvises new approaches, and maneuvers to gain an advantage.
Does not take risks when consequences are difficult to determine or are clearly negative.	Takes risks in spite of potentially negative consequences.
Can repeat the same kind of change without significant learning taking place.	Draws important lessons from change-related experiences that are then applied to similar situations.

D TYPE	**O TYPE**
Reacts to disruption by blaming, attacking, and CYA activity.	Responds to disruption by investing energy in problem solving and teamwork.
Unable to influence others or resolve conflicts effectively.	Able to influence others and resolve conflicts.

IMPLICATIONS

The above list of attributes can be more overwhelming than helpful if it is not viewed in the proper light. Be careful as you assess your own potential for resilience or that of someone else. Resilience is a relative term. When facing major disruption, your objective should not be to display all of these attributes all the time, but to be capable of many of them most of the time. The key to enhancing resilience is learning (or teaching other people) to display as many of these type-O actions as frequently as possible. Any attempt to hold yourself, or others, up to the "walk on water" standard of displaying every attribute all the time would be futile and counterproductive.

Another important implication that can be drawn from the list of resilience attributes is that everyone has both D and O tendencies, but our life experiences tend to mold what we believe to be true and expect to happen regarding change. These beliefs and expectations have a powerful effect on our actions. For example, once people believe and expect to relate to change in a manner consistent with type-D thinking, they maintain that orientation for the rest of their lives unless a concerted effort is made to see things differently.

It is important to note that someone exhibiting a type-D preference is not bad and that there is nothing wrong with resistance to change. Resistance is a natural, healthy response to disrupted expectations. An individual defines his or her personality, and a corporation its culture, as much by what is rejected as what is accepted.

Given the strong human need for control, in certain circumstances, some type-D responses are just as legitimate and appropriate as type-O reactions. In fact, there are many situations where change should be resisted passionately. Problems arise when type-D responses become predetermined, instinctive, and habitual.

CHAPTER 15

ENHANCING RESILIENCE

*I*s it really possible to enhance a person's or group's resilience? How would you actually advance the threshold at which change produces the dysfunctional behavior of future shock? What would enable you to use your assimilation points more wisely and thus reduce the number needed to accomplish a major change?

Addressing these questions, we can draw an analogy between increasing resilience and the issue of whether creativity is an acquired skill or an inherent trait. In the past, many people thought creativity was a gift you either had or you didn't. Most educators now believe that people operate with a baseline capacity for creativity that, if strong enough, can be nurtured and developed into a much more powerful capability.

A key determining factor regarding the amount of ground that can be gained is the level of creativity you start with. People with minimal imagination and inventiveness may not progress as far as those with stronger capabilities in these areas. Everyone can, to some degree, learn how to be more creative. But people who have a high baseline find it relatively easy to enhance their creativity, while others with a more modest baseline capacity struggle to achieve even small improvement.

There is another group of people who can make significant progress in developing their creativity, but only as the result of conscious efforts to exploit the moderate baseline capacity with which they have to work. To do this, they must be willing to learn and apply methods that allow them to replicate the thought and behavior patterns of those with a higher baseline of creativity than their own. By thinking and doing the things more creative people do, you can become more creative yourself.

The same goes for your ability to increase your resilience. Some people operate with a high capacity for increased resilience, some with little capacity for its development, and some with only a moderate capacity. It is relatively easy to increase resilience in people who are predisposed toward it and tough to gain major advances among people with an inherently low capacity. Individuals who have a moderate baseline can enhance its development but only by making a special effort to learn from those who demonstrate stronger resilience. Again, by replicating what resilient people do, it is possible to become more resilient yourself.

Most people who wish to increase their speed of change have developed poor habits that hinder resilience. To break from the bonds of their well-established habits, these people must recognize and learn the mechanisms resilient people apply.

There are plenty of examples of people breaking out of old boundaries that can serve as models, but only if we can learn to recognize them. How is it possible that a weak, gangly teenager can grow tired of being intimidated by bullies and through years of hard work and determination become a world-class body builder? How does a mother overcome her own painful childhood and provide the kind of parenting that promotes healthy, creative, loving children? How can a manager with a long history of operating by mandate and authoritarian rule shift to a style characterized by fostering empowerment in employees and encouraging their participation in decisions affecting their work? These examples have four key elements in common with the challenge of learning how to be more resilient to change. Success in each of these examples requires:

1. An understanding of the prevailing (but unseen) patterns that influence how people operate in certain situations;
2. Respecting these patterns;
3. Conserving assets; and
4. Liberating latent resources.

These four elements also represent what you can do to enhance your resilience or that of others.

UNCOVERING THE RESILIENT PATTERN

Most people think that the outcome of organizational change is due more to luck than anything else. As I stated earlier, the change process can be viewed instead as a structure made up of eight patterns that have predictable effects on how people react to disruption. These patterns represent the typical knowledge, behaviors, feelings, and attitudes humans display when they face circumstances that are significantly different from what they had anticipated.

In the chapters included in Parts III and IV, I described the seven support patterns and identified the principles from each that can be used to enhance resilience. In addition, resilience has its own pattern of operation that is the subject of this and the other chapters in Part V. This primary pattern is the foundation for a person's resilience and consists of five basic characteristics: being positive, focused, flexible, organized, and proactive. By uncovering the hidden dynamics of resilience within this pattern, it is possible to begin removing the cloak of mystery that surrounds change.

RESPECTING THE PATTERN

Respecting the resilience pattern is crucial. I use the term *respect* not to convey awe but to reflect the necessity of abiding by the dynamics that govern any pattern we want to use to our advantage. If you want to negotiate a particularly challenging section of white-water rapids, it is not adequate to simply have a technical understanding of how to maneuver a raft on water. You must respect the river and defer to its power in order to survive and succeed. Only through knowing the river well enough to understand and obey its laws can one safely achieve the desired goal.

In this sense, respect doesn't imply approval. It is not necessary for a manager to agree with staff complaints about the new reorganization plan for the manager to listen to them, understand the staff's perspective, and respect staff members' frames of reference. Simply by receiving respect for its views, the staff will probably feel that the manager's efforts to resolve the issues are genuine.

When we can learn the dynamics that govern its operation, we can use this knowledge to enhance resilience. Becoming proficient in the mechanisms that enhance the resilience pattern means respecting its formidable influence on the success or failure of any change effort.

CONSERVING ASSETS

A tremendous amount of personal, organizational, and societal resources are wasted every year as people struggle against aspects of their resilience pattern that they do not understand and/or respect (e.g., low tolerance for ambiguity, engaging in too many diverse change projects at once, and so on). Many people invest a great deal of their time, money, physical strength, and emotional stamina flailing against these unseen enemies. Relationships fail, companies become insolvent, and governments are toppled due in part to the concealed dynamics that are beyond most people's ability to recognize.

In any aspect of our lives, when previously hidden patterns are decoded, existing resources that the mystery consumes are freed for more productive use. For example, once a person unlocks the pattern that was the basis for her recurring sickness, she can avoid the food source to which she is allergic. The physical and emotional energy that she expended to deal with the symptoms and the lost productivity and revenues that resulted from missed work can all be redirected to more constructive endeavors.

The same is true for becoming more resilient to change. Once you understand the five characteristics of resilience and their respective attributes, the physical, intellectual, and emotional energy that you used to struggle against these forces can be better protected. For example, by failing to recognize how expensive it is when stress in one area of your work spills over into other areas, you can waste a great deal of energy that could have otherwise been available for absorbing change. By compartmentalizing this stress, you can confront it and it does not consume as many of your assets (physical, intellectual, and emotional energy). When you conserve instead of waste these assets, you strengthen your resilience capacity.

LIBERATING RESOURCES

Learning the dynamics of the unseen patterns affecting our lives allows for the possibility of more than just protecting our current assets; the liberation of previously unknown resources can take place as well. When formerly camouflaged patterns are understood, it becomes possible to gain an advantage from the very things that were previously being fought.

One method for treating stuttering is to teach stutterers that part of the pattern from which they are suffering is the result of their own fear. They are afraid that they will stutter, and the subsequent anxiety increases their stress, which promotes their stuttering. The fear of something that they cannot control establishes a self-fulfilling prophecy.

Some patients regain control by intentionally doing what they are afraid of doing. They learn the principle of initiating their own stuttering, but with specific intent. The therapist will instruct the individual to stutter four times—b- b- b- b- ball. Once this is done consistently, the patient moves to three times, then continues to reduce the repetitions until the stuttering is eradicated. The enemy—fear of stuttering—becomes an ally in learning to manage the problem.

Race-car drivers used to avoid the other cars on the track until air-flow dynamics (previously unseen patterns) were better understood. Now it is common to see them use the principle of "drafting," in which one driver exploits the competing car in front to help break the wind resistance and "pull" his car along, thus saving fuel and effort.

Uncovering previously concealed aspects of your resilience pattern means that certain advantages that you didn't know existed can become available to you. For example, one attribute of a resilient person is the ability to reframe a situation, turning seemingly negative circumstances into positive ones. When faced with resistance to a newly proposed reorganization plan, the resilient manager would avoid the tendency to respond in anger or not pay attention to the complaints. Instead, she would see the resisters as providing vital information about their frames of reference, which she could use to either modify her plan or help them see the situation from a new perspective. Her approach would include encouraging the resisters to express their concerns, but not just as a way for them to vent their frustration. Her primary motive would be to genuinely understand and value what they said to gain a new advantage (additional input) toward her ultimate objective. This could only be accomplished by actively listening to their problems.

The benefit of reframing resistance as positive information is a latent resource that was always there but not previously visible to her. The advantage is that she now has a greater capacity to absorb change. She didn't acquire more assimilation points; she simply gained additional points that had not been previously accessible. Assimilation points are not invented; they are liberated.

Michelangelo once claimed that he did not really create the figures he carved in marble. They were already in the stone; he simply chipped away the excess so they could be seen. Over the years as I have watched people learn to become more resilient to change, his meaning has become increasingly clear. The capacity for high resilience is already within each of us; part of the challenge is in learning and applying the techniques to release it.

INCREASING YOUR RESILIENCE

You can gain a powerful advantage by learning the patterns that influence your life, respecting the mechanisms that govern their operation, using this knowledge to conserve existing assets, and releasing additional resources that were previously unavailable.

The gangly teenager learns and respects the psychological patterns of self-esteem and the physical patterns of exercise and nutrition, applying this information to his advantage. The mother gains insight into the parent-child patterns of her upbringing, using this knowledge to understand her own tendencies and emotions and that of her children so as not to repeat another cycle of child abuse. The manager learns to break from the patterns of fearing loss of status and distrusting others and relies instead on the power of synergy with others to succeed during major change.

The process of achieving these transformations is no different from the one required to increase resilience. It calls for developing an opportunity-oriented (type-O) approach to change as outlined in Chapter 14. This means learning to recognize the five basic characteristics of your resilience pattern, respecting these characteristics as vitally important to maximizing your speed of change, using them to conserve your known assimilation assets, and liberating any latent assimilation resources that may be made available.

Strengthening these five characteristics is an important first step to increasing your resilience. You can expand your resilience even more, however, by using principles from the seven support patterns. This is accomplished by recognizing and using the "landscapes" of change.

DETERMINING THE LANDSCAPE OF A SPECIFIC CHANGE PROJECT

To maximize resilience and drive change effectively, the relationships among the various patterns and principles discussed earlier must be viewed in a way that they can be understood and managed. The structure of change provides this perspective and consists of the eight patterns that reflect how people typically react during organizational transitions (see Figure 22).

Although our research at ODR focuses on the primary pattern of resilience, we have found that its full potential can be realized only when used in conjunction with the other patterns. The principles of resilience that emanate from the seven support patterns must be applied in concert with characteristics of the resilience pattern itself.

Think of the five characteristics from the primary pattern as reflecting the baseline capacity a person or group has for resilience to change. When dealing with a particular change, this baseline or foundation of resilience can be augmented by drawing on principles from the other patterns. These principles link the primary resilience characteristics with the support patterns. In doing so, the principles serve as a source of additional resilience strength that can be developed for a specific change effort. The total resilience available for people involved in a particular project is determined by combining the baseline level with any additional capacity generated from the application of the linking principles (see Figure 23).

THE STRUCTURE OF CHANGE

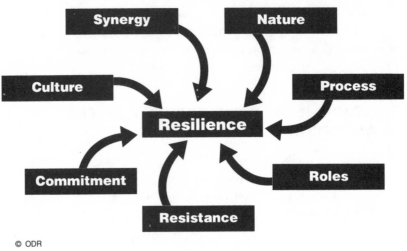

© ODR

Figure 22

Two key implications can be drawn from this chart:

1. The baseline resilience for a person or group may vary greatly from the total resilience level generated for a specific project.
2. The application of select principles from the support patterns can significantly increase the resilience of the people involved in a specific project, as well as accelerate their overall baseline resilience for any future changes.

To reach the heights of change-management effectiveness, you must understand the entire structure of change: the eight patterns, the resilience principles, and the final element—the landscape of change. Let's review and define their functions.

The *structure of change* is a view of the human dynamics of organizational change that reflects the most influential mechanisms and their relationships to one another.

THE IMPACT OF APPLYING
PRINCIPLES TO BASELINE RESILIENCE

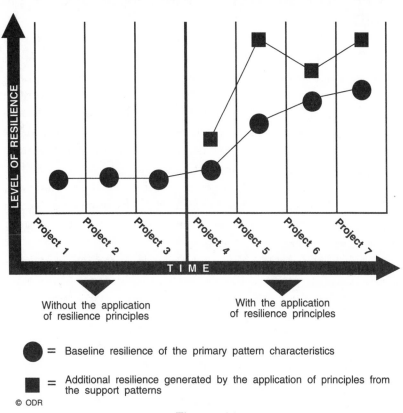

Without the application
of resilience principles

With the application
of resilience principles

● = Baseline resilience of the primary pattern characteristics

■ = Additional resilience generated by the application of principles from
the support patterns

© ODR

Figure 23

The *eight patterns in the organizational change process* represent
the many variables involved when people change within organizational settings. These variables can be categorized into eight
critical patterns. Each pattern represents a category of knowledge, behaviors, feelings, and attitudes people typically display
when facing organizational circumstances that are significantly
different from what they had anticipated.

Resilience is the primary pattern that represents the most important factor for people to function successfully in times of change. The other seven are considered to be support patterns. It is from these seven support patterns that principles are drawn and applied as additional reinforcement to the baseline of resilience in the primary pattern.

The *resilience principles* related to each of the seven support patterns tend to enhance the overall resilience of the people involved, when applied to a specific change situation.

The structure of change for a project is viewed as a constellation of constantly shifting variables (the five resilience characteristics, the seven support patterns, and the many related key principles). In each specific change situation, some of the resilience characteristics, support patterns, and key principles will be particularly important. The configuration of these elements, which needs special attention, is termed the *landscape* of a change, and represents the points of influence that will have the greatest impact on resilience.

The landscape of a change reveals the intersection of characteristics, patterns, and principles that can be used to enhance a person's or group's overall resilience strength. A landscape view of a specific change effort consists of:

- the support patterns that appear to be particularly important to the project's success; and
- the linking principles from these patterns that would be most helpful in maximizing available resilience.

Rather than a static, one-dimensional "snapshot" (as if suspended in time), a landscape view of change captures the motion inherent in constantly shifting variables. Sometimes the fluctuations among the variables are as subtle as the interaction of clouds moving slowly across the sky. Other times, the shifts in their relationships to each other are as blatant as churning waves in a heavy sea.

When these forces merge and interact, they form a configuration unique to that situation at that time. Due to the dynamic nature of these shifting variables, the length of time a particular landscape's configuration is stable is roughly twenty-four hours. To recognize and properly use the most important characteristics, patterns, and principles for a specific change demands vigilance throughout the life of the project.

USING LANDSCAPES TO ENHANCE BASELINE RESILIENCE

The way the landscape of any particular change forms is dictated by the degree to which the key sponsors, targets, agents, and advocates demonstrate type-O characteristics and can adhere to the resilience principles from the seven support patterns. A significant modification in any one of these support patterns or a slight alteration in a few of them could dramatically influence the final outcome of a project. As an example, even if all the other variables remain constant, a project's success hangs in the balance if either sponsorship commitment falters or synergy between two key groups is strengthened.

There are situations in which a single characteristic from the resilience pattern in combination with only one principle from one of the support patterns could make a fundamental difference to the outcome of a change project. For instance, a senior officer of one of the large consumer products companies in the United States told me of his experience during a year-and-a-half-long effort to dramatically reshape the structure and culture of his organization. He said that the time and effort he and the other senior executives had devoted to the task was well in excess of anything he ever imagined would have been necessary or possible. Restructuring the company and shifting its culture were, of course, tasks to be completed in addition to the already demanding day-to-day requirements of just keeping the business running. Yet he reported that he and the other senior staff members performed better under these conditions than at any time since they had worked together as a team. He said that it was a grueling experience, but one that taught him and most of the others that they possessed more individual and collective capacity to deal with change than they had realized.

When I asked to what he attributed this newfound resilience, he said that for him one of the most important type-O characteristics was viewing life as positive and dynamic. The attribute from this characteristic he tried to consciously reinforce in himself was the notion that no matter how well he and the other senior executives planned their actions, the future would be made up of constantly shifting variables, and they were therefore going to be routinely surprised at the actual turn of events.

He described himself as a reformed binary thinker who spent much of his career being caught off guard, getting angry, and blaming others when his brilliantly conceived plans did not always materialize as he expected. He confessed that the ambiguity of such situations was terribly uncomfortable for him and so, despite years of his plans never fully matching reality, he continued to cling to his rigid planning process and the belief that "This time, they will get it right."

He said, "Looking back, I wasted a great deal of my own energy and the company's resources trying to hit that home run that doesn't exist. After learning how this kind of behavior was reducing my own resilience and the company's too, I made a conscious effort to prepare for the unexpected as we progressed with our change project."

He described how difficult it was for him as a black-and-white thinker to engage in the paradox of preparing for the unexpected. Even after overcoming the intellectual struggle of such a shift, he said that he still found himself sometimes not knowing how to apply what he now believed that he should: "I had particular difficulty in learning to anticipate the inevitable resistance that takes place with major change. My saving grace was a lesson that I learned from one of the principles out of the resistance pattern. The principle is that positive as well as negative change produces resistance and each has a sequence you can use to predict behavior." He went on, "One of the lessons I learned from that was that during positive change, uninformed optimism always precedes informed pessimism. Once I had the principle and the lesson it supported as guides, I could become much more prescriptive with myself about how to avoid wasting my resources fighting against the inevitable. I think the company and I are much more resilient today because of this."

This situation shows how one implication from one principle out of one support pattern, when used to reinforce a single attribute from the primary pattern, can have a dramatic effect on a person's or company's overall resilience. The landscape elements important to this example are as follows:

LANDSCAPE ELEMENTS

Key Resilience Characteristic	Positive: views life as challenging but opportunity filled
Isolated Attribute	Expects future to be filled with constantly shifting variables.
Critical Support Pattern	Resistance Pattern
Principle Drawn from the Resistance Pattern	People facing major change are more resilient when they understand that resistance to positive change is just as common as resistance to negative change, and that both reactions follow their own respective sequence of events, which can be anticipated and managed.
Lesson Taken from the Principle	Uninformed optimism always precedes informed pessimism.

The graphic on the next page depicts how this particular combination would look if seen as part of a landscape view of the situation. From the resistance pattern, a single linking principle reinforces the strength of the person's overall resilience.

This is an example of only a small portion of the dynamics inherent in a major change effort. There may be many people involved. For each person there are five resilience characteristics that individually or in some combination may prove important. There are seven support patterns. For each support pattern there

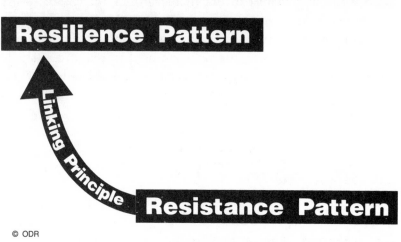

Figure 24

are one or more resilience principles that may be used to strengthen the primary resilience pattern of any one person or group. The number of possible combinations that might be influential to the outcome of a particular change effort is formidable.

Thank goodness not all of these variables are relevant all the time. Winners are people with the ability to identify which of the many variables are, at a given time, important to orchestrate in order to achieve the desired result. A landscape view of how the critical characteristics and linking principles are interacting with each other sheds light on what must be done to maximize the amount of resilience that can be attained among the key players.

Only by raising our level of resilience can we successfully assimilate the increasing rate of complexity and ambiguity in our lives. To help accomplish this, we can use these landscape views as a means of picturing the fluid nature by which the structures of change actually unfold during a specific project. Even though these landscapes are constantly shifting, it is possible to keep up with what is happening and even influence the outcome if the variables are seen as definable characteristics, patterns, and principles that can be understood.

Recognizing which landscapes hold the key variables that will increase resilience is not enough. These variables must be acted upon. That is, the structure of change must be managed: The right linking principle(s) from the correct support pattern(s) must be matched with the appropriate resilience characteristic(s). Only when this action is taken can you consciously enhance the baseline strength of your own or someone else's resilience.

MANAGING THE STRUCTURE OF CHANGE

In summary, managing the structure of change for a specific project is accomplished by:

- determining the level of baseline resilience that exists among key people involved in the change;
- identifying which of the seven support patterns will provide the greatest leverage for the desired outcome;
- recognizing which of the principles from these support patterns can be most useful in reinforcing baseline resilience; and
- applying the correct resilience principles with the appropriate resilience characteristics to bolster the basic strength of an individual's or group's overall resilience pattern.

Part VI

OPPORTUNITIES AND RESPONSIBILITIES

*I*n the future, the world you consider now to be so disorganized, irregular, and convoluted will appear by comparison relatively stable. Whether the time horizon you envision is five years or five generations from now, change-related crises will be more frequent and more complex than today. History tells us that regardless of the magnitude and intensity of these challenges, some people will emerge as winners while others will lose ground. Many people will view their lives as so chaotic that they will consider their very economic, emotional, or physical survival in jeopardy. Yet in the midst of this same turmoil, others will appear much more grounded as they maneuver to seize advantages made possible because of shifting circumstances.

The people who survive and prosper during times of great change are the individuals, groups, and societies who learn to take advantage of the mechanisms that foster micro, organizational, and macro resilience. The opportunities in store for those who are resilient are abundant. But along with these opportunities come definite responsibilities.

CHAPTER 16

THE ETHICAL PLOY

We all know that deception is bad. Fraudulent snares confirm our worst fears about people who try to covertly manipulate others to achieve their own selfish desires. Nevertheless, there are certain ways in which we attempt to influence one another that involve an honorable form of masquerade. By this, I mean that there are circumstances that justify disguising one's ultimate intent when seeking to persuade others; I call these efforts to influence "ethical ploys."

An ethical ploy is at work when one person grants another's request to do something but fulfills the obligation in such a way that the recipient not only gets what was promised (the ethical part) but also has an opportunity to gain a great deal more than was requested (the ploy). These honorable deceptions are used to lead people into seeing a point of view to which they otherwise would not have been able or willing to relate.

Ethical ploys reflect a belief that sometimes the best way to help people develop a new perspective is to use their existing frames of reference rather than fight against them. For example, refusing someone's request for help because you believe that he is asking for the wrong thing often leaves that person angry and alienated. These feelings typically reduce your chances of further influencing him. By granting his request for help, you can demonstrate an acceptance of his perspective. Feeling accepted usually lessens his need to defend his position and increases the likelihood that he will listen to new views.

If someone asks for your advice regarding how to confront an employee about his poor performance, you have an opportunity to not only grant the request but also to help that manager see how she may be contributing to the situation in some way. This approach is a form of virtuous trickery because of your wish to go beyond what was asked of you and to add value where it was needed but not solicited.

The ethical way to deal with these situations involves first offering some straightforward guidance regarding exactly what the manager requested.

Manager:

This guy is driving me crazy. He submits sloppy work and is always missing his deadlines. What do I have to do to fire him without getting into a lawsuit?

You:

I would recommend that you document your concerns and be specific about the incidents that demonstrate the gap between your expectations and his performance. Feedback is not considered by the court to be helpful to people unless it is given in a manner that provides concrete examples. Also, be careful not to imply anything about his intent. Someone's motives about doing or not doing something can be difficult to prove legally. It's usually best to stay focused on documented behavior.

Something else to consider is whether or not anything you have been doing could in some way be influencing his behavior. For example, I've learned in the past that some poor performers who worked for me were not executing their duties properly because I had not provided adequate training or meaningful incentives. I found that by not doing these things I was adding to other difficulties the employees were experiencing and aggravating their performance problems.

Worse yet, on a few occasions I realized that my failure to appropriately train and reward had been the primary reason that they were doing so poorly on the job. These are not things you want to be vulnerable to during litigation. In fairness to the employees and to protect yourself, you should carefully examine both his contribution to the problem and yours.

The manager's request for assistance is to accomplish only one thing—termination of the employee without triggering legal action. Offering any other advice without addressing that issue first would have probably been met with resistance. By granting what the manager wanted in a way that also raised additional, unsolicited issues, a window of opportunity opens for the manager to broaden her perspective on the situation. But she may or may not understand, agree with, or take action on the new frame of reference being offered.

An ethical ploy does not overtly force or covertly manipulate anyone into thinking or doing anything. It simply addresses issues or information that would otherwise not be seen, understood, or considered relevant. It is a way of opening doors, not pushing people through them.

This is an honorable approach to influencing others for three reasons: First, it demands that you do exactly what you agreed to do. Second, it requires that you believe that the new perspective you are promoting represents a positive opportunity for the person. That is, even though there may be advantages for you if she accepts the new viewpoint, your motives are not purely self-serving. You are honestly offering something that you believe is in this person's best interest. Third, it dictates respecting the person's right to not be ready or willing to accept your point of view. The ethical safeguard in such an approach comes from delivering what you promise, having the person's best interest at heart, and not coercing him or her if your views are not accepted. The ploy is to guide people toward the possibility of a new journey by leading them down a familiar path.

Although the term *ethical ploy* may be new, this approach to influencing others is familiar to almost everyone. Most of us use this technique all the time but usually on an unconscious level. We may, therefore, not be as careful of its potential misuse as necessary. Ethical ploys are potent ways to influence people, and so it is important to remember that the task is to fulfill your agreed-to obligation while exposing, not coercing, people to new interpretations of what they normally see.

The more emphasis you put on the ethical aspects of this technique, the more powerful your ploys can be. As long as you are able to meet other people's needs and respect the sovereignty of their viewpoint, the likelihood that you can meet your own agenda of changing their minds increases.

Once people feel their needs are being met, you can be more direct about your intentions without offending or appearing to be pushing your viewpoint. The key when using ethical ploys is to remember that in spite of how passionately you believe in your own frame of reference, others will not come to accept your views unless they are ready to do so.

When using an ethical ploy to enroll other people into your viewpoint:

- Be clear about what you want to accomplish.
- Identify what the people you are trying to influence want to achieve.
- Promise to provide some aspect of what they want.
- Fulfill this obligation exactly as promised.
- Expose them to a new perspective.

After applying an ethical ploy, be prepared to either seize the moment if people should gravitate toward your advice or accept that their readiness for doing so or your reframing skill is not up to the task.

THREE PLOYS

This book discusses the use of ethical ploys on many different levels. In the following section, I will discuss three examples to highlight the concept of enticing people in an ethical way to see more than they expected from a situation.

Organizational Learning Applied to Life

Change creates a crisis for people when it invalidates their expectations about important issues or events. We already face more of this kind of crisis than we can effectively absorb, and even more is expected in our future.

While we must address all three types of change—micro, organizational, and macro—many of the best learning opportunities for developing resilience can be found in organizational arenas. The ethical ploy here is in teaching people how change can be managed at the office in a way that also exposes them to the personal and societal applications of the same principles.

To enhance our quality of life, we must each assimilate the growing burden of change without displaying so much dysfunctional behavior. But there are few opportunities to work on organizational projects entitled "Advancing the Quality of Life for Today and Future Generations." What leaders do express an interest in are ways to bring to their organizations structure and predictability as the world grows more chaotic.

By helping managers learn and apply the dynamics of change, it is possible to help them accomplish what they are seeking—and more. They can learn to implement reorganization plans, new technology, quality-improvement programs, or key acquisitions in a manner that dramatically reduces unnecessary resistance and significantly increases commitment to implementation success. Nevertheless, learning these skills also creates the possibility that leaders may become aware of application opportunities beyond the organizational setting.

The Hidden Benefits of Synergy

Another honorable ploy in this book has to do with synergy. We all need to learn to relate to each other more effectively. It is alarming to witness the mounting misunderstandings and conflicts among the diverse individual perspectives and cultural norms represented in today's workplace. The same divisiveness can be seen in many stressed families, in strife-torn countries, and between belligerent governments. Our collective inability to respect and creatively use diversity significantly reduces the speed and effectiveness with which we can assimilate change.

If we are to succeed in turbulent times, we must deal with each other in a manner that fosters a value for diversity. This is best done by working together synergistically. Yet to position synergy within some kind of "mom and apple pie—do the right thing" framework would severely limit its ability to influence most senior managers. Most executives expect their sermons and philosophical lessons to come from church or a university, not their place of work. From the business environment, leaders simply want to know what will help make their organizations more efficient, effective, and profitable.

I did not, therefore, portray synergy in this book as the newest way to show humanistic concern for workers. Instead, I positioned it as an approach to managing diverse viewpoints to generate maximum productivity with minimum consumption of assimilation resources. Synergy is also a mechanism that fosters creativity, empowerment, and participation, but that is secondary to the primary business reason it is applied in most situations. The face value of synergy for most managers is that it produces more output with fewer resources, thus increasing an organization's overall resilience during change.

The "ethics" associated with promoting this type of teamwork relate to the overwhelming evidence that synergy truly helps people achieve more with fewer resources. The "ploy" is in helping people see that there is an alternative to the $1 + 1 < 2$ or $1 + 1 = 2$ equations of human interaction. The prevalence of self-destructive and static relationships in the work setting does not result from human nature. We are in these types of relationships mostly because of poor teamwork habits and ignorance. For many people, these are the only type of work relationships they have ever known. Our objective should be to help them realize there *is* an alternative.

No Panaceas

A third example of how I have attempted to use ethical ploys deals with the illusion of "home runs." A question I raised earlier in the book was: "What would happen if we received what we said we want?" What would it mean if the organizations that influence our lives were capable of successfully planning and executing changes? What impact would it have if these institutions were skilled at not only making the right decisions about change at the right times but could also successfully implement these decisions? How would our lives be affected if the various bureaucratic formations that serve, govern, control, direct, guide, council, influence, educate, heal, protect, inform, and motivate us were capable of achieving their change objectives on time and within budget? What if organizations actually did become more resilient?

The answer to these questions is that increased resilience represents both an opportunity and a danger. The best way we can take advantage of the former is to be aware of the latter.

The opportunity of resilience can be summarized in one word—*hope*. Without the ability to increase our resilience, we would face a doom-and-gloom future of more change that would be increasingly difficult to absorb and would result in escalating dysfunction. With the knowledge that we can learn to understand and manage what in the past has appeared mysterious, new options become available that make us hopeful and excited about the kind of world we and our children live in.

Demystifying the change process generates a capability beyond avoiding future shock. By approaching change in a disciplined manner, we can become architects of our future. Increasing our resilience will enable us to release our creative energy to invent new possibilities, which would have previously been unthinkable!

The application of resilience principles can be used as a powerful competitive advantage for any organization facing major changes. The same approach and techniques used to create change opportunities in the organizational sector can also produce advantages for individuals dealing with micro change (marriage) and for large groups of people contending with macro adjustments (overhauling the American educational system).

Yet resilience is not a home-run panacea that will alleviate all our problems without also producing dangers. Increasing resilience within the organizations that affect our lives is a powerful solution to the threat of future shock, but it is not an elixir without side effects.

Becoming more resilient represents a major change itself with its own set of consequences. Are we as a society better off since we began using cars and planes as our primary means of transportation? Yes and no, but mostly yes. Modern forms of transportation have both given us much and cost us dearly (air pollution, for example).

Gaining a greater capacity for organizational resilience is no different. We must take this step in learning to build more resilient organizations, but to do so will again increase the complexity of the world we live in. Let's not forget what happens when you get what you pray for—uninformed optimism is always followed by informed pessimism. Rather than pretend that this second stage does not exist, we can increase our chances of success if we will "soberly sell" ourselves and others on resilience as a core value and skill for our future. That is, we must celebrate the benefits that increased resilience will help generate while we prepare ourselves for the inevitable invoice that always comes as a companion to major, positive change.

RESILIENCE RESPONSIBILITIES

I hope you are able to apply many of the concepts and approaches outlined in this book to benefit both your career and your organization's prosperity. Yet because of the accelerating volume, momentum, and complexity of change, and the tendency people have to identify themselves more as victims of their circumstances than as architects of their destinies, the application of the resilience lessons presented here represents something beyond opportunities. These lessons also entail certain responsibilities.

If it is possible to actually uncover some of the mysterious patterns that guide human behavior during change and intentionally raise the resilience level of people facing transition, shouldn't we do it? Once managers have been exposed to how winners deal with institutional transition, shouldn't they prepare their organizations for the advancing demands of change? After realizing that transitions can be managed in an architectural fashion, shouldn't world leaders apply such approaches to the large-scale changes inherent in many of their decisions and policies?

By focusing this book on patterns and principles that managers can use to implement successful organizational change, I hoped to move beyond this legitimate but limited value of enhanced resilience. My wish is that readers will embrace a wider responsibility that consists of long-term, more ambitious objectives. Organizations serve as useful and appropriate forums for the application of resilience, but if our knowledge is used only at work, the necessary quantum leap in humanity's capacity for assimilating change will not be significantly affected.

For just a moment, accept that the principles you have read about here are truly capable of helping people implement major organizational change more effectively. What would you do with the information? Would you attempt to apply some aspect of increasing resilience to your own work setting in the hope that you could gain a competitive advantage for your career or your organization? I certainly encourage you. But what next? What other organizations that affect your life could benefit from a higher threshold for future shock?

Beyond the organizational applications, whom do you know who could gain an individual advantage if he or she knew how to manage better his or her own emotions and behavior during a transition? Are you interested in social issues that affect large constituencies? Is it possible for a disciplined implementation approach to play an integral role?

Starting at home you can begin by teaching your family how to manage change. But the insights you learn in your micro world can also help you on the organizational level, and the learning you gain managing organizational transition can help you be of greater service to your church, local community, or country. Successful change management is not merely an opportunity to dramatically improve organizational performance, it is a responsibility we all share for making our personal lives more effective, our countries more competitive, and the world a healthier place to live.

Whether for ourselves, our families and friends, our companies, our church, our local community, our country, or the whole planet, successful change management represents more than opportunities. It also reflects a responsibility to apply what we know.

TO PAY THE PRICE

There's a *Peanuts* cartoon that features a dejected Charlie Brown with his head in his hands and a "sigh" in the bubble over his head. The caption reads, "There's no heavier burden than great potential." Reading this book may have generated the same feeling in you. Applying what you now know about managing change will bring you a special potential. The price for this knowledge is a corresponding responsibility not only to use it wisely but also to master the techniques that make well-executed application likely.

This mastery is not likely to be acquired by reading alone. To expect mastery without great effort is to misunderstand what you are seeking. True mastery of any skill requires the patience and dedication of a serious student. If you are a serious student of change, you will study the patterns of change and principles of resilience, practice the skills needed for their application, acquire the discipline to apply those skills despite frustration, and demonstrate a devotion to the task that will sustain the effort for many years.

Some people who read this book will not feel compelled to apply what they have read. Some will have a desire to use the concepts, but only occasionally and not with any depth.

Others may become highly motivated to master the resilience principles in order to tackle the burning-platform challenges of the micro, organizational, and macro changes facing us now and in the future. Through their efforts, it will be possible to continue to develop our understanding of the mechanics of resilience to be better prepared to face day twenty-nine and keep the lily pads from choking the life out of our lake.

Today, we desperately need skilled people who can bring structure and discipline to a changing world. The mythical beast that terrified me as a youth stalks millions of others throughout the world and personifies dysfunctional reactions to a world in rapid transition.

Taming the Beast is essential to enjoying the benefits and avoiding the pitfalls of our future. The Beast prospers in our ignorance when we view transitions as mysterious, inexplicable events. The key to successful transition rests in identifying and using the dynamics of change that lie just below the surface of our awareness. This requires learning the patterns of human behavior and the resilience principles that make up the landscape of the changes we face.

Enhanced resilience must be our objective, and learning its

dynamics is a mechanism for reaching this goal. The patterns and principles that comprise resilience must be approached in a flexible but disciplined way for them to be applied consistently and in a manner that empowers others to avoid future shock in their lives as well.

These are not easy goals to achieve, but the alternative is prohibitively expensive. We will either pay for learning how to manage change at a speed that will accommodate the transformations that face us or we will pay for not doing so. Regardless, we will pay. The opportunity to choose which option is collectively ours, but the responsibility to act is personally yours.

EPILOGUE

....

In 1974, ODR, Inc. was formed as a research and development company dedicated to the study of one phenomenon—how people respond to major change. Although most of our work has been conducted in organizational settings, the purpose of our research is to determine what contributes to human resilience in any setting. Our goal continues to be the construction of methods and procedures that foster the conscious development of resilience in individuals, organizations, and whole societies.

Despite our gains over the years in demystifying the change process, identifying what winners are doing to successfully implement change, and isolating what we believe are the key components to resilience, there is much work left to do. In fact, I am more humbled by how much we have yet to uncover about human change than proud of what we have learned. From this standpoint, it would be premature to present this book as the definitive statement on change and resilience. I hope you view it instead as an interim report that will require additions and edification in the future.

What I have offered here are some of the lessons and insights I have gained from my many years as a participant and observer of the process of human transition. These findings should be considered both preliminary and suspect, however. They are preliminary because nineteen years is not a long time to study a phenomenon so complex, and suspect because, although our research involves as much quantifiable work as possible, we also rely heavily on field observations and interviews. As such, our findings are susceptible to all the difficulties associated with any subjective analysis of human behavior. Nevertheless, if you will view the results I have reported here as reflecting the "art" as well as the "science" of managing change, I believe you will find genuine value in their contents.

Because there is so much more to be learned about how resilience can be developed in our personal lives, professional work, and social architecture, I would like to extend an invitation to anyone who believes he or she may have something to contribute to this endeavor. If as you read this book you thought of a personal experience, organizational situation, or large-scale social phenomenon that reinforces or refutes any of our findings, we would be interested in hearing from you. If you are involved in any type of formal or informal study related to human resilience, we would be eager to exchange ideas. If you are attempting to implement major change in a unique setting, in an unusual way, with extremely large groups of people, or if you are expecting to face extraordinary challenges, we would be enthusiastic about establishing an ongoing dialogue or correspondence with you to remain current with your observations and learnings.

In some ways, ODR functions like a small university with only one field of study in its curriculum. Once people have been exposed to our latest findings regarding resilience and organizational change (whether through publications such as this book or formal training programs conducted by ODR), we encourage them to consider themselves alumni and to participate in the "resilience brain trust." This brain trust is made up of people interested in furthering their understanding of how humans can better absorb major change in their lives. Hundreds of people from all over the world now participate in this brain trust by offering perceptions, insights, and techniques that result from their own experience with change. We at ODR are constantly field testing these ideas to determine which ones have universal application potential. Once a year, the findings from these field tests, along with the results from our own independent research projects, are incorporated into the format we use to apply what has been learned—Managing Organizational Change™ (MOC™). MOC is a set of flexible but structured procedures designed to increase individual and organizational resilience while successfully implementing major change. All those who belong to the brain trust receive a summary of the annual revisions to the MOC methodology so they can benefit from the ideas offered by the others who participate.

If you or your organization would like to become a participant in the resilience brain trust, you may contact ODR:

By phone: 1-800-CHANGE-U

By fax: (404) 455-8974

By letter: ODR, Inc.
             Product Development and Research
                Department
             2900 Chamblee-Tucker Road
             Building 16
             Atlanta, GA 30341

Please call 1-800-359-1935 or write to:

Mentor Media
1929 Hillhurst Avenue
Los Angeles, CA 90027

for information on the videos
Managing at the Speed of Change
and
Resilience: A Change for the Better

ABOUT THE AUTHOR

....

DARYL R. CONNER is the founder and CEO of ODR™ Inc., a research and development firm dedicated to the study of human resilience in organizational settings. Based in Atlanta, Georgia, since 1974, ODR has trained thousands of people in the United States, Canada, Latin America, Western and Eastern Europe, South Africa, Asia, Australia, and the former Soviet Union in the use of its disciplined approach to implementing major transitions.

The combination of Mr. Conner's master's degree in psychology and his extensive consulting with major corporations, governments, military leaders, nonprofit organizations, educational and religious institutions, and public school systems throughout the world has provided him a depth of experience with change that is matched by few people. He has written more than sixty publications, including journal and magazine articles, monographs, and chapters of books on the subject of change management. His international recognition as an authority on the human aspects of change generates a constant demand for his speeches, training seminars, and presentations to various management development forums.

He is married with two sons, and the Conners divide their time between homes maintained in Atlanta and New York.